SECOND TIME AROUND

SECOND TIME AROUND

From Art House to DVD

D. A. MILLER

Columbia University Press

New York

Columbia University Press
Publishers Since 1893
New York   Chichester, West Sussex
cup.columbia.edu

Library of Congress Cataloging-in-Publication Data
Names: Miller, D. A., 1948– author.
Title: Second time around : from art house to DVD / D. A. Miller.
Description: New York : Columbia University Press, [2021] |
Includes bibliographical references.
Identifiers: LCCN 2020025092 (print) |
LCCN 2020025093 (ebook) | ISBN 9780231195584 (hardback) |
ISBN 9780231195591 (trade paperback) |
ISBN 9780231551397 (ebook)
Subjects: LCSH: Motion pictures—Reviews. |
Motion pictures—Technological innovations.
Classification: LCC PN1995 .M5255 2021 (print) |
LCC PN1995 (ebook) | DDC 791.43/75—dc23
LC record available at https://lccn.loc.gov/2020025092
LC ebook record available at https://lccn.loc.gov/2020025093

Columbia University Press books are printed
on permanent and durable acid-free paper.

Printed in the United States of America

Cover image: Still from Max Ophuls's *La Ronde* (1950)

It can't *be* like the first time. Something's happened.
—*Double Indemnity*

What can you see? What can you see now?
—*The Passenger*

CONTENTS

CONTENTS

SECOND TIME AROUND

PART I

SECOND THOUGHTS

"I WOULD ADVISE every older scholar to tell his public the basic experiences underlying his methods."[1] Thus spake Leo Spitzer, the great philologist famous for his focus on the little details that make up an author's style. For some time, I have been old enough, male enough, and in the right profession, to consider myself directly addressed by this invitation (standing since the year I was born), but I never had any inclination to accept it. My idea of the experiences that determined a critical practice—or any adult commitment, for that matter—involved far more basic events than the academic course of study to which Spitzer, not taking his advice very far, proceeded to reduce his own method's origin story. Even supposing I could fake his assurance, I was too skeptical of his reliance on voluntary memory to think that I should ever retrieve, between my method and my experience, any link of real importance. But suddenly there came a point when I understood that this method was no mere method for me; it was also, and had always been, a sort of design for living. It didn't just have certain select life experiences *behind* it of the kind Spitzer was enjoining me to recount. It was itself a way of telling—and reflecting on—my entire life story, and that story was ongoing. Throughout my professional career, I had apparently been doing one of two equally perverse things: either I had been secretly writing autobiography in the alien mode of criticism, or I had been cynically strip-mining my life for the sole sake of ever-finer hermeneutic discriminations. The ambiguity needed articulating—and whether I declaimed in Spitzer's amphitheater, or whispered in the alcove where criticism is now conducted, or just talked to myself at home like a crazy, my acoustics could stand improvement.

"But suddenly there came a point": the point at which I reread the contents of this book. With these short DVD reviews (all but the last written for my *Film Quarterly* column called "Second Time Around"), I had turned my writing to a new subject and a smaller scale, and like going abroad or looking at miniatures, the retrospect revealed habits that were too natural or contours that were simply too large to have been recognized before. At the outset, only one such discovery needs to be shared: namely, that I tend to imagine my critical work as a series of *returns*. Sometimes, quite literally, I have returned to authors and texts more than once: my multiple Austens, Bartheses, and Hitchcocks. But sometimes, even though I am writing on a subject for the first time, I set it up *as* a return: here is *David Copperfield*, for example, or the Broadway musical— old familiar things about which I am now having (unnerving phrase if ever there was!) "second thoughts." And sometimes the subject keeps coming back without even being named in the uncredited form of frequent, always shifting allusion: hidden Poe, hidden Kinbote. The "Second Time Around" column, full of returns to old art films, is itself the return of a column I wrote on then new art films as a Cambridge student. In sum, almost all my writing has proceeded under the beleaguered assumption that *everything needs to be done twice.*

And why? Because it wasn't done properly to begin with! It is as if everything I write is a sort of repair work, an attempt to revisit a somehow fractured (spoiled, disparaged, lost) first encounter, whether to fix it or, failing that, to affirm that I have survived it and am ready for a second round. But this repair work, in laying bare the old impairments, shames, and privations, never quite lays them to rest but seems instead to invite further repair work . . . on itself! We know from Proust that the second trip to Balbec is as disappointing as the first, but—here's the rub—it's disappointing *in different ways.* I, too, seem incapable of imagining I'll ever get a visit right.

But if you've read many first-person narratives, or even tested a few online dating profiles, you'll know to be wary of those who tell their own story. Feel free to read a different one between the lines; I, too, will be telling other versions of the second-time narrative as this book goes along. But I tell it this way first to justify the present introduction, which *I have written twice.* The first time (in "The Cinematheque Today," which follows) I simply attempted to post, as forcibly as possible, my Lutheran theses regarding the new cinematheque and its typical DVD reissue. But by the end of it, I found myself wanting to write it over, this time (under the title "The Second Time Around") as a reflection not on my subject matter but on myself as a subject in relation to it. For my early passion for watching films—and art films, in particular—was a passion in the double sense, divided between an acceptable enthusiasm and a more intricate secret suffering, and that split provided the main impetus to see them—and to write about seeing them—a second time. My Janus-faced introduction will make explicit the poles—objective and subjective, critical and confessional—between which, in a continuing attempt to abolish the opposition, the columns oscillate.

1. THE CINEMATHEQUE TODAY

YESTERDAY. By the *old* cinematheque, I mean not just the Palais Chaillot in Paris but the whole transatlantic aggregate of film societies, festivals, archives, art houses, and private homes where the religion of cinema was practiced during my youth. For whether performed in a major basilica or a recusant chapel, the liturgy came down to the same single sacrament: the projection of a film that was *hard to see*. Hard to see because prints were precious few and points for distributing them were equally sparse. The film might not always be the opus of an auteur, but it invariably was a rarity; the showing might never be repeated. But hard to see, as well, because the film was in a visible state of rot. Your eyes were always straining to puzzle out the palimpsest of the original film that lay dimly discernible under a dense patina of dirt, lines, snow, and scratches or that had to be surmised from mutilated, censored, stolen, or simply missing frames; you soon got used to a print catching fire before your eyes. And hard to see, finally, because, after all, "hard-to-see-ness" is built into the very nature of film. People speak of "catching" a movie, but the moving image is intrinsically on the run and always outpacing the eyes that would chase it down. We are not catching the film so much as losing it, again and again, as one frame displaces another.

The film culture I acquired at the old cinematheque, in other words, was woefully full of holes. My coverage, worked up in an economy of scarcity, betrayed enormous, ignominious gaps. The images were themselves half-buried in another kind of hole, under an irremovable thick overlay of aging and neglect. And through still another hole, the narrow aperture of memory inevitable in watching any film at all, my retention of an image would start to slip as soon as the one after it came on screen. The details I didn't immediately forget, though monumentally vivid for standing out on the mnemonic flatland, were approximate at best; sometimes, on a rare second chance, I'd learn I had made them up. But I submitted willingly to these hardships, never doubting that I followed the true faith, much less abandoning it for the laxist multiplex, where the movies were brand new, easily accessible, and perfectly soulless. And yet, as the years passed, my practice lapsed despite itself: churches that celebrated the sacrament, fewer everywhere, had vanished from my vicinity; those hard-to-see films had become impossible to see. If by then I had reached midlife, my cinephilia, dominated by reminiscence rather than observance, was already in full dotage.

■ ■ ■

TODAY. Then, with the suddenness of a revolution, there sprang up a new cinematheque—a cinematheque without tears, without the regrets of evanescence—that eliminated all three varieties of hard-to-see-ness at one fell swoop. This new cinematheque, conveniently headquartered in my own apartment, puts at my disposition not only every movie I'd seen at the old one but also every movie I'd missed seeing there, and all of them in mint condition to watch whenever and as often as I please! More and better, I now hold the reins of a viewing contrivance that lets me check every dubious memory—decelerate any teasingly too-rapid sequence—demonstrate the suspected connectedness of far-away frames—and in general perform all those retrievals once merely wished for but now realized as routine functions: pause, step, forward, back, slow, fast, skip, grab, bookmark.[2] *Remote?* What an egregious misnomer for the device that grants me a fantastic *intimacy* with the film image, which I can now manipulate from only a couple of feet away. Nor does *control* seem quite the right word for a tool that I use not to subdue a film but to be further transported by it. This is not the weapon of my will so much as the vassal of my whims—of random associations, casual or ancient obsessions, and other unruly impulses that come from my un-, pre- and semiconscious states. Hardly remote—but not wholly in hand either—the film-on-disc invites a deeper surrender to the image even in the promise of an increased mastery.

Given my devotion to the old-time cinephilia, I ought to be astonished at how immediately—and with how little regret—I embraced the new rite. I can only assume, as Natasha says to Andrei in *War and Peace*, that I had been waiting a long time for it. Like everyone who falls on the right side of a revolution, I have no patience with nostalgia, least of all my own, for the precedent era. I accept the brutal sacrifice of luminescence, grain, the grand scale, and a sense of audience—the immolation of everything that used to distinguish the authentic experience of cinema from movie watching. And I do that for the sheer luxury of, say, spending five hours watching an old film from 1960 that, with a running time only half that, used to pass by too fast for me. On this weird new adventure—in this weird new *L'avventura*—I go anywhere and everywhere to track, if not the missing Anna, those once fugitive film images that her sudden disappearance and failure to return had allegorized for me, and when, as often happens, I find one of these images especially arresting, I *let* it arrest me and go nowhere. Raymond Bellour might say that, without projection and an audience, I have forsworn looking at cinema as such, and certainly I watch at close enough quarters to be mindful of the conversion of film's look into oversharp and oversaturated digitality. But the truth is nonetheless that my absorbing hours of close viewing in the new cinematheque have given me the most intense experience of cinema in my life, though it may not strictly be cinema that I am watching; never has my involvement been so immersive, my exposure so porous. And occasionally, as an emblem of this unprecedented intimacy, I spot the reflection of my face—pallid and preempted—superimposed over the image on the computer screen as if the film and I were dissolving into one another. This state of suggestion, in which I am wholly open to the image, eager to follow up its innumerable leads but having no preordained point in doing so, has become the desired pitch of my movie watching.

■ ■ ■

TOMORROW. The cinematheque of the future? I envision it, drearily, as the lengthening shadow of datedness falling over the cinematheque of today. Technology has foreseen the obsolescence of both the DVD and its distinctive viewing practices. The insert slot has disappeared from my new computer, along with the step and bookmark functions in the player application. And the emergent streaming technology makes it onerous-to-impossible to deviate from the straight line of cinematic unspooling; could theatrical hard-to-see-ness be coming back as home entertainment? Soon enough, I imagine, my habits of close viewing, already thus straitened, will bear the epitaph of their historical closure: "During 1997–20xx, this is how some people enjoyed cinema!" But in the meanwhile? The decline of an era is said to release its fiercest energies. It would be unduly pathetic to be enjoining myself to "seize the day" at its twilight; instead, I take my motto from the time after sundown ideal for viewing: "The night is still young!"

■ ■ ■

CLOSE TO, TOO CLOSE. The essays in this volume rehearse a common template. In each, I watch a newly released DVD edition of an art film I saw—somewhere—on the old cinematheque circuit. Inevitably, it's then versus now: my potent, if patchy, memory of the film contends with the harsh precision of its recaptured images. But the contest is uneven: it is the present moment that affords me the opportunity I've been waiting for, the chance to make up for old privations, and so my emphasis falls decisively on this "second" encounter with these images, which I put under the minutest inspection that DVD technology allows.

The aberrancy of this inspection cannot and should not be finessed: my attention is so much closer than common understanding is felt to require that, to many, it may look as if I've abandoned the project of understanding altogether. Even to me at times, my orientation to small details feels no different from wandering lost and lonely among them. The filmic *hard*-to-see, I find, hasn't been abolished by the new cinematheque so much as dialectically assimilated in the digital *too-much*-to-see. Overwhelmed by the superabundance before my eyes, I feel I might as well be seeing nothing—nothing that matters, at any rate. For that is the notorious drawback of seeing an object close to: the object loses its legibility; it has got too close even for the modest comfort of meaning, let alone that sumptuous state of meaning we call importance. It is meaning in any state, of course, that serves as the default for all our acts of looking; it is the glaze on our gaze that prevents us from seeing anything that isn't simultaneously saying something. We keep being told that ours is an image culture, heir to the dominance once enjoyed by word culture, but it is nothing of the sort. The very idea obscures an altogether different state of affairs, in which rampant verbal captioning shrinks our images into easily understood—and circulable—abstractions. Our so-called visual culture seldom leaves the purblind scope of its deep-seated antivisual bias.

I notice, for instance, that the highest form of image in mass culture—the apotheosis every image aspires to—is the *icon*: an image that, by dint of being recognizable at first sight, hardly needs a second glance. No less symptomatic is a recent academic call to *surface read* the image, where *surface* designates an image's transparency to truth and *reading*—as anything more than simple assent to self-evidence—is openly deemed superfluous. And I pass over the dark day when film studies substituted "the archive" for face time with the film image. Everywhere in the culture the thing to see is busily being eclipsed by a thing to say about it. Both things become trite in the process, which is perhaps the point of so vigorous an exercise—to grant us a universal dispensation, in a world that is frankly going mad, from the need to confront anything seen or unforeseen.

But nowhere, for my purposes, is the battle, as I still prefer to think of it, between image and word more relevantly waged than in the very format of a DVD reissue—in its constitutive split between the *restoration* of the film, with its bracingly unfamiliar images, and the *commentary*, a feature that lets you supplement the audio track with a lecture, in which a denizen of that just-mentioned archive talks over these images, figuratively as well as literally. My assessment of the combatants follows.

■ ■ ■

BATTLE OF THE DVD I: THE IMAGES. Arrayed at one end of the arena stands a phalanx of images, whose power—particularly

on this second time around—should by no means be under-
rated. Scrubbed and brightened, they are riveting in their raw
new nakedness; for all their smallness, they are photo-realisti-
cally sharp; and even their shrunken frame, harder to forget *as*
a frame, has the advantage of wonderfully compacting them.
Their unsettling brand-newness, which makes them in some
cases look younger than on first release, repels all nostalgic tendency to dwell in the *Casablanca*-like fog suitable for misty eyes
and hazy memories. Even a higher-toned Proustian recovery
seems hardly feasible; here, in principle, is the past recaptured,
but it breaks spectacularly with the past we remember. In this
respect, the rejuvenated images wear a faintly mortuary aspect,
as if a certain life, the life we'd lent them, has been taken out
of them. But whether by their new strangeness or by our new
estrangement from them, we are startled to only greater attention; not just unremembered but even, it seems, unremember-
able, these images catch our eye more forcibly than ever before.
"Don't for a moment think," they seem to say, "that you know
us already or can dismiss us as old acquaintances with a passing
nod. You're going to have to look at us now, not just 'again,'
but *as for the first time!*" Such peremptory self-importance is,
literally, in our face; if it is difficult to deny the cogency of the
challenge, it is easy enough, with some curiosity of mind and a
remote in hand, to accept it.

■ ■ ■

BATTLE OF THE DVD II: THE COMMENTARY. Opposed to
these images at the other end of the arena, the commentary

restrains their force by two main tactics, one involving content and the other form. It is striking, as to content, that, though the commentary talks over the images incessantly, it never talks about them. The neglect is definitive. Far from confronting the *allure* of the images it is synced to, the commentary reduces them to mere triggers, reminders of one or another item in the mere *lore* it passes down instead. Background on story and production, snippets of star or auteur biography, narrative summary, gossip from the set, anecdotes from the premiere, timeless themes, deathless factoids—these, and no more, are what the visuals cue the commentary to purvey.

Such lore, being half-mythological to begin with, goes down more easily than knowledge. There is nothing the least bit forbidding about the commentary; it is as affable as the open-collared academic typically chosen to deliver it. Some signs of erudition, conveyed by a hard word or two, may be necessary to confirm the film's, the commentator's, or our own distinction, but otherwise the commentary courts accessibility supinely. This means, practically, that whatever ideas we receive from it must be *idées reçues* before a word has been spoken. We must have heard the commentary's generalities about the Weimar period or the economic miracle before; the game plan counts on that. And we must also believe that we could find all its other points, if we bothered, on the internet; the game plan counts on that, too, as amounting to a conviction that, when it comes to accessing the status quo of "what people say" on a subject, this lecture is every bit as current as Wikipedia.

Our foreknowledge of what the commentary has to tell us, in short, can only assist in its appointed mission to stamp the film with *banality*. If it's thus stamping the film for the second or for the umpteenth time, well, then it's an even surer bet that we will be acceptably blasé the next time it comes up in conversation. Even when, on occasion, the commentary indicates "a famous shot," it lets us know only that the shot is well known; additional remarks on the shot's construction or composition would be fatal to the work of imprinting. And so it goes. By the commentary's end, nothing has been looked at, but everything has become familiar. We have been turned into the idiot savant who, asked if he's been to the Louvre, says, "No, but I've heard of it."

That the commentator is often a brilliant scholar makes clear that the problem inheres not in aptitude or preparation but in the form itself. If a commentator *did* want to talk about the images, the constraints of this form would simply not allow it. For the commentary must be coterminous with the film that it audiotracks; the information it imparts, shoehorned or dilated, must fill that duration precisely. Inevitably, such necessity turns every commentator, no matter how compelling elsewhere, into the worst sort of chatterbox, talking throughout the entire film and jumping from topic to topic, unable to dwell on any for longer than the brief screen time of the image that is (if nothing else) its prompt. Hence this cruel structural double bind: the commentator is required to be long winded but is forbidden to expatiate. Notation takes more time than the image has to give; it is possible, in other words, only when the image can be stopped, slowed, enlarged, compared. Oddly behind *its own times*, the DVD commentary refrains from the very operations that its auditors may accomplish as a matter of course. It doesn't simply refuse the DVD's new visuals; the better to do that, it also rejects the pedagogy implicit in the DVD player's new ways of seeing them.

■ ■ ■

"THE COMMENTARY IS MY ENEMY!" In what I've called the battle of the DVD—really a battle for the DVD—I am a decided partisan. But it is in detail that I best like to fight. The polemic conveyed in my close viewing is quite simple: it consists in observing, again and again, in case after case, some striking *failure of transparency* in the film image, a marked resistance to the immediacy of our knowing what we see. Here I discern an internal incongruity that damages the coherence of the image as a whole; there I notice how badly the image fits the narrative or ideological slot the film has prepared for it; and everywhere (not just in relation to an individual commentary) I encounter what might be called the image's vocation to exorbitancy, its intrinsic tendency to exceed the verbal accounts provided of it. "It's not a word thing," says David Lynch of film. Put under close watch, the image will seldom fail to reveal how regularly even rigorous verbal descriptions fall into imprecision, omission, error, amnesia, contradiction, and other forms of untruth. The details that I bear down on, accordingly, are not microcosms, meaning's big pictures in little. They are not even oddly shaped keys that nonetheless succeed in "opening" the work (which surely always means sealing it up like a tomb). They are fracture points in the image's presumed obviousness, and as such, they put the glib flow of meaning on pause. The pause, while it lasts, returns the activity of interrogating the image to the center of film understanding.

NOTES

1. Leo Spitzer, "Linguistics and Literary History," in *Linguistics and Literary History* (Princeton, NJ: Princeton University Press, 1948), 1.

2. I initially explored these functions on two optimal testers, the first being *Psycho* (1960) and the second a Jeff Stryker porn film called *Bigger than Life* (1986; not to be confused with—but, of course, ribaldly resignifying— the 1956 Nicholas Ray film of the same title). Hitchcock's shower scene, slowed and paused, became more fascinating to observe than ever. But, given pornography's fundamental exhibitionism, applying the retarding functions to Stryker felt like bringing coals to Newcastle; the film was already geared toward letting you see—more than once and for as long as possible—everything. Here the accelerant functions—fast, skip—came into their own.

2. THE SECOND TIME AROUND

THE FIRST SECOND TIME. Until I turned fifteen and could go downtown on my own, I had almost no chance to see a film more than once. Rerun opportunities were rare in the 1950s, and though there must have been *someone* who went back on Sunday after a Friday opening, it was never anyone in my family. Why on earth would you want to see a movie that *you had already seen*? The question would be posed as though no answer were possible; the sheer idea bespoke the indulgence of those, unlike us, with nothing better to do. It never occurred to my parents, or other relatives who took me to the movies, that if they liked a film, they might simply—with no tax on their frugality!—remain in their seats and see it again; even when, having arrived late, they were obliged to stay into the second show to see what they'd missed, they would pop up like dolls on a spring at the precise point we had come in.

But their abstemious ethic of "once and no more" may have testified to the very strength of the temptation to linger under the image's spell. Certainly, what I say didn't occur to them occurred to me all the time, and in my desire to prolong the stimulation a movie had given me, I'd often turn back to the screen to catch a few second seconds as I was being taken out of the theater. Being impossible, however, my desire for "a second time" could never have entered that ordinary living room in which I often put a favorite song on the record player or reread a familiar story; being impossible, it had to be relegated to the psychic subbasement—small, cramped, depressing to visit— where all my more or less shamed quixotisms lay drugged like abducted children. In this captivity, a grandiose desire to win a newspaper contest and a desperate hankering to be Ronnie Thornton's best friend kept company with (the first example I remember) an aching desire to rewatch *Pinocchio.*

For one of my generation, television might have been an easy means to see movies twice—at least the old Hollywood ones—had not a similar domestic repression prevailed here too, daytime TV being laid under the same embargo as late-night programming. I sometimes attempted to set up a sort of Pleasure Island at my grandmother's house, where the TV, always on but never watched, was mine to do with as I liked. Planting myself in front of the set, the better to see (already a four-eyes!) and be near the dials, I would sample the forbidden fruit of daytime TV: soaps, game shows, Garry Moore, and Hollywood movies from the thirties and forties. My truancy was disappointing, not at all like smoking, playing pool, or suddenly sprouting a donkey tail (excitements to come later in life), and the movies on offer (I remember *Comrade X* and *A Midsummer Night's Dream*) bored me fully as much as *Queen for a Day* and Bert Parks.

But one memorable late afternoon I found myself watching a movie, a thriller, that grabbed me at the start and held me all the way through. I watched it so raptly that if there *had* been a thought of seeing it again, that thought was already keeping Ronnie company in the fruit cellar. The next day, at the same time, I returned to the TV in the modest hope that I might see something in a similar vein to the film of the day before. What I found was not in the same vein; it was the same film, unfolding on the screen as in the simplest species of dream. And while my eyes were absorbing the visual evidence, my ears took in, during a commercial break, the no less astonishing information that, by the same miracle of programming, I could watch this film again on the following afternoon, which I did, and on every afternoon until the end of my visit to Nonna's, which I did as well.[1]

I make two observations about this, my first "second time." The first is that I experienced no difference between my successive afternoon viewings; the breaks between them were as negligible as the commercials within them. I was the same David Albert Miller on Thursday as on Monday, and *Dial M for Murder*, still trochaically scanning his name, was the same film, shown on the same TV at the same hour; it felt, each time, as if I were simply reentering, with no change in, much less diminution of, intensity, a single mystical ecstasy. And the second observation bears on the kind of knowledge I did and didn't acquire in this paranormal state. Nonna's mingy black-and-white TV set—not even a console!—would have obscured the

film's structure had I been curious or competent enough to ana-
lyze it. But I was not seeking illumination or a film education,
only a perpetuation of the enchantment I was under. In any case,
far from assisting my understanding of the film, these repeated
viewings succeeded only in permanently disabling it, in the way
that repeating a mantra empties its words of meaning. In most
people's judgment, *Dial M* is an ordinary murder mystery, a
"thin" Hitchcock, but to me, it remains so hypnotic and (probably on that account) so incomprehensible that it might as well
be *Last Year at Marienbad*. If anything, these repeated viewings
only tightened the coils of its spell, eliminated any shred of my
resistance to it.

Yet as is well known, one does strange things under a spell—
performs prodigious feats that one could never achieve, would
never attempt, in waking life. Though I understood *Dial M* no
better on Thursday than I had on Monday, by the end of the
week, with the memorization skills of youth but no conscious
intention of exercising them, I knew its dialogue by heart. *Faute
de mieux*, I had seized upon the almost unbroken talkiness of
the film as an expedient whereby I could reconjure everything
else about it as well. This odd source of intimacy, long ago sup-
plemented by a DVD, has not been supplanted. Let a psychi-
atrist ask me who Margot is or Tony, or why I am so invested
in having her murdered and him move out of their bedroom;
all I know is that, simply by reciting certain lines then learned
by heart, I once again go into my old enamored trance. Even as
I write this, I hear Tony saying to Swann, with particular apt-
ness to my case, "You used to go to the dog-racing, Mondays
and Thursdays; I even took it up myself just to be near you."

That is all my first second time did for me: it got me nearer the love object. But that is all I seemed to want.

■ ■ ■

DATES, INTERVALS. I note, for the dozen-plus films I write about here, the following information: the year of the film's original release; the year and place I saw the film for the first time; the year in which, on TV, VHS, or DVD, I first saw it a second time; and the interval between first and second viewings:

> *Sansho the Bailiff* (1954 [U.S. 1969]). First time 1969, New York City; second time 2007; interval thirty-eight years.
> *Cruising* (1980). First time 1980, San Francisco (showing picketed); second time 2007; interval twenty-seven years.
> *Berlin Alexanderplatz* (1983). First time 1984, Berkeley, CA; second time 2007; interval twenty-three years.
> *Bonnie and Clyde* (1967). First time 1967, San Francisco; second time 2008; interval forty-one years.
> *Pierrot le Fou* (1965). First time 1968, Paris; second time 2007; interval thirty-nine years.
> *Rocco and His Brothers* (1960). First time 1967, Yale Film Society; second time 2003; interval thirty-six years.
> *Vertigo* (1958). First time 1958, San Francisco; had the second time been the theatrical rerelease in 1983, which I saw several times, the interval would have been twenty-five years, but it wasn't: I saw *Vertigo* for the second time in 1966, on black-and-white television at my parents' house,

while, during the commercials, I attempted to make a transformer for physics class; interval eight years.

La Ronde (1950). First time 1970, college film society (not sure which), Cambridge; second time 2008; interval thirty-eight years.

The H-Man (1958 [U.S. 1959]). First time 1964(?), black-and-white television, my parents' house; second time 2009; interval forty-five years.

La Femme infidèle (1969). First time 1969, New York City; second time 2003; interval thirty-four years.

Toby Dammit (in *Spirits of the Dead*, 1969). First time 1969, New York City; second time 1998; interval twenty-nine years.

Le Beau Serge (1958). First time 1971(?), Paris; second time 2011; interval forty years.

Medea (1970). First time 1972, Cambridge Arts Theatre, Cambridge; second time 2011; interval thirty-nine years.

The Birds (1963). First time April 4, 1963, opening at the Golden Gate Theatre, San Francisco; second time April 13, 1963; interval nine days. Sudden death of family norms, precipitous birth of cinephilia.

■ ■ ■

THIRTY-FIVE YEARS. Roughly speaking, my first viewing of these films occurred soon after their original U.S. release, while my second took place thirty-five years later. The first time around, the films were coeval with my youth; even my excursions into the cinematic past (Ophuls, early Chabrol) were then as fully "happening" as the cinephilia whose dictates I followed in making them. By the second time, however, these movies had long ceased to lay claim to the new and now, and even if *they* had reemerged looking unbelievably well-preserved, the benefit of digital deaging was not extended to the surviving cinephiles who had watched them during the 1960s and 1970s and who, like myself, had now entered sixties and seventies of their own.

It's a long, steep flight of years that takes you from the twenty-fifth station of, say, Young Man to the sixtieth station of Older Gentleman; by the end of the ascent, your breath is short, your knees wobble, and your soul seems to be bearing as many spots as your skin. But the climb, however injurious, is said to be character building, and when you turn around to look back on all you've risen above, you are promised a prospect superior to anything you've seen before: the view from Maturity. What's more, lest your failing sight tempt you to equate this ascent with its antithesis—with sheer decline—waiting to assist you with their incomparably powerful lenses are those classic works of art you had long promised yourself to put into service at just such a moment. The fact of the matter is that I *do* attain this mature perspective every time I am recovering from an accident or surgery and pick up some great novel I haven't read in decades. The author's understanding of human nature seems more profound than ever as I corroborate it from the augmented store of my own. And in confirming the novel's truth, my existence (normally wanting in any obvious principle of organization) acquires the shapely coherence of fiction and even some of its appealing pathos. The back-and-forth persuades me that, in growing old,

I have grown up. I tell myself with confidence that I have lived a full life or, more simply, that what I have sustained for so many years *is* life, the real rich ripe thing known to Tolstoy, to Proust, to Murasaki, and now at last to me!

But something quite different—more irritating, and therefore perhaps actually more *like* life—befell me when after a similar long intermission I returned to the art films of my youth. Even if I had foreseen this return, of course, I would no more have expected such works to reconcile me to later life than to return me to youth; they are about the dissonances of experience, not the harmonics, and you'd hardly revisit them to take the waters, reparative or nostalgic. But neither did I expect that—in their brand-new look, too!—they would oblige me to suffer afresh, with no abatement of distress, the oppressions I felt on first watching them. For devoted as I was to the art film, it used to scare me; as soon as one began, I'd feel my stomach knot up as if, by means of *Persona, Blow-Up, Teorema, Contempt*, or *In the Realm of the Senses*, I had got into a kind of trouble there was no getting out of. And now, in defiance of the long passage of time—as though it were a vacuum in which I had done, seen, learned nothing—the antique anxiety had returned not only with all its old bite but further magnified by this evidence that, as a spectator, I hadn't passed beyond it. In the brand-new home theater, no twilight performance of maturity was likely to take place; the principal was indisposed. Contrary to the assumption in the song from which this book takes its title, I still did not have "both feet on the ground."[2]

■ ■ ■

NOT GETTING IT I. In youth, my torment was of two orders. The first was cognitive: I never could understand what I was looking at. Had I been a philistine, it wouldn't have mattered that I was also an ignoramus; but though I couldn't comprehend, I desperately wanted to and sat through film after film, intent on their images but failing to receive the illumination I sought and others seemed to find in them. In contrast to Hollywood movies, whose ingratiating air of spontaneity masked a rigorously structured legibility, the art film, though flaunting the deliberativeness of every shot and image, insisted on its fundamental opacity. I had to get by in a country where urgent information was being conveyed to me in a language impossible to understand. Meaningfulness abounded, but meanings were in short supply.

I obviously do not mean by this that I took no account of the copious critical discourse—reviews, essays, interviews—that any art film spawned then as now. On the contrary, just as someone might ask an astrologer to predict the future, I would pore over that discourse beforehand to learn what I should see, understand, or admire when in the presence of the film itself. Out of it, I fashioned—three decades, mind you, before the DVD supplement—a sort of commentary that I would mentally play over the film much as English subtitles were run over the dialogue. But of all the ideas crammed into my head when I entered the auditorium, not one could I repeat as my conviction on leaving it. For when I attempted to apply these ideas to the images passing before me, either of two things happened. If I held the ideas uppermost in my mind, the images grew silent, noncommittal, and uncooperative, while if I concentrated on the images, the ideas felt glib, remote, and obtuse. On the one hand, the images seemed ill-suited to embodying the ideas, which, on the other hand, seemed all but useless in expounding the images. Never did the thing to say and the thing to see join in the disclosure of "meaning" or "importance" that I was seeking. Insecure even of my confusion, I often felt that the fault lay not in the too-taciturn images or the overabstract ideas but in myself who, looking too intently or in too literal-minded a fashion, was doomed to miss the connection that others, going with both kinds of flow, ideational as well as visual, had no trouble in establishing. All this made the art film a trial to watch, and if I regularly took part in the postfilm conversation with my fellow cinephiles, cravenly pretending that the astrologer's predictions had truly come to pass—if I carried such imposture to the point of writing a student column in which I pronounced with authority on new releases by Antonioni, Bergman, and other famous auteurs—this was all done to dissimulate my embarrassment at having nothing to say.

■ ■ ■

NOT GETTING IT II. This was not the only realm in which I was not at home. Roland Barthes once sarcastically compared the desire for textual revelation to a schoolboy's dream of "seeing the sexual organ."[3] I am not sure these are quite the same thing or are experienced in the same psychic register, but it is certain that, as a Ruskinianly repressed schoolboy, I came to art cinema, then synonymous with "the foreign film," pursuing two kinds of education. I hoped to be inducted into avant-garde artistic practices, and I hoped to behold orgies worthy of Tiberius on Capri. Knowing this cinema largely through our family newspaper (the one that sponsored the contests), I'd gathered that the most acclaimed foreign films were also those that incurred, somewhere in Italy or Ohio, prosecution for obscenity; if they were not actually seized or cut, the projector lamp would be ordered dimmed for modesty's sake. And more often than not, these masterpieces would turn up, in between *And God Created Woman* and *Viridiana*, on the Legion of Decency's condemned list, radiating what the Legion liked to call "unmitigated license."

Too excited by this perennial scandalousness to doubt the claims on which it was based, I was convinced that "filth" was as intrinsic to the art film as foreignness; it was dirty and difficult in equal parts. As such, the form promised to be a useful hybrid of high culture (my aspirations) and pornography (my dreams). And as if to bear me out, not long after I began my attendance at the old cinematheque—at no less significant an initiation than a viewing of *Persona* (Surf Theatre, 1966)—my schoolboy's dream almost immediately came true in the shot of a tumescent cock. It was the first erection not my own I had ever seen, and like those, it had come without warning. But I'd been banking on it for years! Combined with the cryptic montage in which it was embedded, it set before my eyes, in all its obscene but unintelligible reality, the bona fide art cinema I'd been imagining since the dawn of puberty.

The shot, though, was a prick-tease. It lasted just long enough for me to identify the hard-on but not long enough for me to look at it. It barely met porn prerequisites, let alone the needs of the story, in which it never recurred or got explained. That, no doubt, left only symbolism. At the Ciné Café afterward, my best friend, Billy, suggested that Bergman had proposed the cock as a *phallus*—sign of all that the film's two female protagonists would form their relation around and against. But his hypothesis irritated me as much as the shot. This furtively exposed cock made a sad excuse for the paraded phallus, and the very evocation of "the phallus" made an even sadder excuse for the uncushionable shock of an erect sexual organ. In a word (but oh! this word I was too timid to utter), the elision of desire made our whole conversation the saddest excuse of all for an experiment we never conducted.

I only appear to digress. The art film didn't disappoint me as a sexual being so much as draw out the already absurdly long delay in my becoming one. Those *films à scandale* I used to read about—once in addition to motive, I finally had means and opportunity to see them—did not liberate, clarify, or goad to action. On the contrary, they were mere reverberators of my own sexual confusion, partners in the inhibitedness from which I had gone to them hoping for release. Certainly, sex was one of the art film's favorite themes and pushing the frontier of sexual representation its frequent project, but the expression of these commitments was invariably entrusted to a far more insistent aesthetic of *tact*, a discretion whose key formal constituents were fragmentation, cutaways, high-speed montage, slow pacing, static frames, long shots, extreme close-ups, off angles, and distracting music. It was as if a barker had promised me a naughty sideshow of "interpretive dance" and I then spent two hours behind the curtain watching—stripped of nothing but its quotation marks—interpretive dance. Or as if the ultrasophisticated art film had set out to mimic the diffident, gap-ridden sexual imaginary of a Catholic schoolboy with nothing yet to confess.

Sex in the art film might well be idyllic, incoherent, stately, tense, modern, pensive, or perverse—might boast a dozen other *serious* attributes of sexual experience. But it was never clear, precise, blunt, gross, intractable, straightforward, or any of the other lowdown things also proper to that experience. Time and again, just when a film seemed about to arouse or educate me, it would retreat into beauty: the beauty of a face, a landscape, a composition. The naked bodies would become silhouettes, the breasts sand dunes. That was the art film's routine legerdemain: on the brink of being sexy, it turned itself into something lovely to look at, a liquid cleared of all sediment. In this, too, I suppose, it was like me, who, in lieu of being sexual, became an aesthete fond of art films. In running against the Hollywood norm, my strange connoisseurship was the only minoritization I admitted. And yet, at the moments when the contrast between my ugly desire and its radiant replacement was most extreme—for instance, when *Persona's* head-rearing cock gave precedence, in the same opening montage, to the beautiful faces of Bibi Anderson and Liv Ullman being sinlessly caressed on a movie screen by a bookish boy in spectacles—my aestheticism felt as painful as my chastity.

■ ■ ■

THERE ARE THOSE WHO BET: THE WAGER. These were the two aspects of the anguish that broke out again whenever

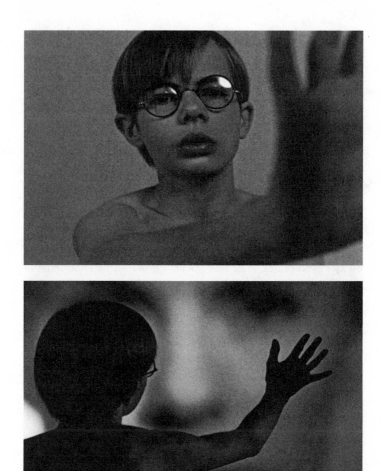

Ugly glasses, beautiful spectacle.

I opened a jewel case with certain European or Japanese "gems" inside. It was as if I'd simultaneously unlocked a strongbox in which I had formerly stored that old feeling and now found it as good as new. Worse: nothing else was in the box! It hardly mattered that I now knew French, Italian, and some broken Japanese or that I had advanced in cinema literacy and was better versed in the masters of modern thought; the film image still seemed obdurately opaque in relation to the word or the idea; I would *never* understand how it worked. And despite decades of valiant promiscuity elsewhere, so long as I was in front of a screen rewatching *Les Amants* or *La dolce vita*, I continued my life as a curious but frustrated virgin, equally sensitive to sexual intimations and exasperated by their lack of follow-through; how *that* worked, too, I would always remain too young to know. And yet the sheer insistence of this anguish, as enduring as the films themselves, made it impossible to regard either the emotion or its source as "childish things" to be consigned to a strongbox once more or to a garbage bin for good; I now knew that, if I didn't stay with these things—as, after all, the DVDéothèque was practically begging me to do—they would abide in me nonetheless.

At this juncture, I made myself a wager. Recalling Proust's hypothesis that "adolescence is the only period in which we learn anything," I determined to rewatch the digitized old art films as if my renewed frustrations were not obstacles to my understanding of them, to be cleared away with time and effort, but rather no more or less than *that very understanding*. No purpose, then, could be served in continuing to mask (be embarrassed by) my "nothing to say" until something came along.

Instead, I needed to draw from that nothing its exegetical value, to elucidate the ways in which it was telling the truth, not simply about me but also about that other hermeneutic and erotic disappointment which was the art film. I would have to elaborate my anguish, in other words, beyond the subjective mode I have been adopting here (a mode I regard as less narcissistic than just plain skittish, fearful of realization in the world). If my anguish carried a point, I had to find that point in the objective tensions of the films themselves, and the autobiography of a spectator needed to change into an act of film criticism.

■ ■ ■

THE FATE OF CLOSE READING. *Criticism*—the very word was like a bell! For some things *had* befallen me in those thirty-five years, the following being most relevant:

(1) I had become a critic (academic, literary, mainly of the nineteenth-century novel), and my criticism consisted in close engagement with texts. Though I'd certainly gone to the right addresses for literary study that way inclined—the Jesuits, Yale, Cambridge, Yale again—any other institutional trajectory would likely have produced the same outcome, since in those days close reading was the master technique of literary studies everywhere, the idiom in which even one's most comprehensive or abstract ideas would be rendered.

(2) But with the passage of time—an uneven passage that made the change feel as gradual as thinning hair and as abrupt as a heart attack—there arose other schools of criticism that,

protesting against the authority of the Text, claimed the rival patronage of linguistics, history, theory, sociology, the digital, identity, and so on. In the resultant sectarianism, the lingua franca became a dead language, its former universality surviving only in the general fondness for writing (again and again) its obituary, or unmasking (one last time) its ideological obscurantism, or recycling it ("not your grandfather's close reading") as a mandatory new fad that poor, pushed-around graduate students had to acknowledge or abandon all hope of entering the profession. But, of course, I just misspoke: the lingua franca did not become a dead language; it became an *undead* one, as universal as ever but now, to use a quaint locution of the interregnum, under erasure.

(3) Not that I had any lamentation to make over the departed glory years; on looking back, the close readings of the New Critics struck me as mere motif studies in disguise and those of the deconstructionists as hardly more than the well-wrought urns of high theory. Close textual engagement had certainly brought forth prodigies (Barthes, Booth, Derrida, Empson, Johnson), but in its garden varieties, it looked as automated as the critical machines that replaced it and that a rear guard was condemning in its name. But there was another, more fundamental reason that I regarded this as a world well lost. The clerical utility of close reading had blunted my sense of the *lay* function it fulfilled in my life. Now that the practice was no longer wanted on the job, I could appreciate it as having been, off the job, my most resorted-to spiritual exercise. I still found myself turning to it daily, as others might turn to prayer or an Ignatian *examen*: it was basic to my existential getting-by. By way of quick explanation,

let me recall a diligent, but utterly indifferent, student who thought that a minute attention to the text of *Madame Bovary* was good for nothing but my assignments until the difficulty of another kind of text, sent by a lover to his phone, immediately turned him into a rabid adept at reading between the lines. For it is on such occasions that close reading comes into its own, as a technology for enunciating—for contemplating, expressing, advancing, enhancing, suffering, mourning, surviving—the relation of intimacy. Unlike those spiritual exercises that attempt to *free* the soul from worldly enmeshments, close reading was my habitual resource for engaging the terms of my stickiest psychic *attachments*—to works of art, other people, daily life, affairs of the heart, anything that, for good or ill, got and stayed under my skin.

(4) With this sense of close reading as a professionally shaky but personally unshakable enterprise, there came a change in my critical practice. Was I *still* doing close reading, lighting the lights in an empty motel? No, I was doing it *again*, this second time with a will, an insistence greater than any rationale I could have invented to justify it then or now. In its new phase, my practice, growing wild and perhaps morbid, owned its compulsiveness, like a tree whose roots had come to the surface. Having lost its former commonality, it embraced its fate as an idiosyncratic too-closeness, preoccupied with details at the expense of the whole. I just couldn't look hard enough. I say "look" because I'd also moved away from literary study with its bibliocentric injunction to produce holistic readings. My so-called close *reading* no longer deserved the name; it deserved a better one, more fitting for the extraordinarily congenial object that, with perfect timing, the world had just put under my eyes. This new

object was not film, which always went by too fast for me, but film on DVD, which I was able to scrutinize to the limit.

(5) Thus, by the end of this twisty history, the close reader had become a too-close viewer, and the professional had become, for all his critical training, an amateur.

■ ■ ■

AMATEUR. "No footnotes, no jargon," my editor at *Film Quarterly* insisted at the outset: no academism. Now and then I chafed and cheated, but on the whole, these were congenial strictures. Naturally, some debatable assumptions were holing up behind my apparently self-standing detail work, and a certain type of highly intelligent academic would discern and dispute them. But I was willing to be exposed in that way: it was the cost—and perhaps the proof—of espousing, within criticism, any species of unguardedness. In my student column, I did my best to be a know-it-all; in "Second Time Around," I tried to be a do-it-yourselfer, to match my home entertainment with a sort of house-made criticism. I do not belong to the field of film studies—indeed, I am what the less generous in that field might call a *poacher*, someone with no legitimate claim on the subject except hunger and want. But *n'exagérons pas*: my amateur project is not much of a threat now that film studies has taken the close analysis of individual films off the table; this poacher is catching only game that its lawful proprietors no longer care about. As a kind of viewing that *everyone can do*, it has ceased to interest, much less to be of use in consolidating, a guild of specialists, which has changed its entry requirements accordingly.

But it is precisely as "what everyone can do"—as the province of the laity—that I advocate its practice. Obviously, it would be better to have the Lafayette analyzer, print archive, and screening room that the great film scholars still command, but the minimal new tool kit into which such luxuries have been shrunk has the advantage that everyone may use it. My readers have access to the same down-market technology as myself; the column's regular injunction to "watch with me," accompanied by a DVD chapter reference, lets them find every image I point out and use their own eyes to verify or disprove what mine have found in it.

More: fellow close viewers may watch with me, but even in doing so, they are bound to follow their own initiative. Watching on DVD or via streaming is a case in which everybody likes to go their own way, *and everybody does, willy-nilly.* The new technology did not call into being the infinity of things there are to see in a film, but thanks to the slow, pauseful, nonlinear, and often randomized viewing that it facilitates, it lets us see more such things. And there is something radical in the individuality that this boosted responsiveness can't help expressing. For out of all the little things you have noticed, as if they were magic beans in a fairy tale, there unexpectedly springs up a giant landscape, with spectacular ridges, folds, canyons, monoliths, mesas, and pathways broad as boulevards or faint as lost trails. Though it's like nothing else you've ever seen, this landscape has the archaic, familiar feel of a dream. But of course it does: it is the topography of *your singularity as a viewer.* Though any given detail you single out may have been seen by countless others, a sufficient number of such details single out *you* as their observer: they configure the system (or an image of the system) of *what you alone can see*. Hence, like landscapes in a Western, this one is essentially desolate: the mirror of your solitude. But hence, too, like those same landscapes, it is essentially aesthetic: the mirror of your particular "way," your psyche's art. I said earlier that I sometimes see my face reflected in the monitor while I am close-watching a movie. But it is not my face, or even my personhood, that I find refracted in these amassed details of my attention; it is an object more intimate and more opaque, hard to recognize and so much harder to talk about that I must simply conclude by naming it for my readers' consideration: I glimpse my *style*, that obscure other means by which I continue to write autobiography, even when I am just seeing things.

NOTES

1. How this recurrent programming came to be remains mysterious, abiding in my psyche as pure wish fulfilment. Some who grew up in New York recall a program called *Million Dollar Movie*, which would repeat the same film for a week; did I see a provincial knockoff?

2. Sinatra as ego ideal? "The Second Time Around" (Sammy Cahn/Jimmy Van Heusen) was recorded by every self-respecting sixties vocalist, but Frank Sinatra put the memorable stamp on it. He recorded it in 1960 as the first 45 for his own label, Reprise, whose apt motto was "to play and play again." Then, as if taking a cue from the lyric, he recorded it a couple of years later for the album *Sinatra's Sinatra*. Growing up in a family of fans (Italians on my mother's side, musicians on my father's), I learned to fuss over the minor differences between the two versions. Which had the better phrasing, the 45 or the LP? Did Nelson Riddle significantly enhance his original arrangement when he conducted it himself? Was "what led us to this miracle" more euphonious than the original "what brought us"? But, most basically, what about the first version, which I loved, required doing over?

Around this time, it so happened, I saw Sinatra perform the song at Cal Neva. This rendition, hard to focus on in the noisy and unpleasantly adult atmosphere of the casino, was certainly *not* lovelier; next to the purity of the studio recordings I'd enjoyed, "Sinatra live" was, in more ways than one, a corrupt text. And yet with his unparalleled expressive gifts, that exquisite hypersensitivity that would also, when he couldn't bear it any longer, turn him into a complete brute, Sinatra channeled the dissolute circumambience—after all, "those who bet" were everywhere around him—as the lyric's new context; highball in hand, he gave the words a gruff, coarse, "stupid" utterance, as though he were ventrilo-quizing someone in his audience who hadn't known love, loveliness, or middle-aged wisdom as anything but convenient self-deceptions he was marshaling to launch yet another. Its mystique thus darkly laid bare, this "Second Time Around" acquired an irony worthy of Flaubert; I hated it.

I saw Sinatra only once after this, at Radio City at the end of his career and near the end of his life. The rickety old man in front of me, roughly his age, was uncontrollably thrilled when the singer came on stage: "He looks great, just great!" he announced to those of us around him. I wouldn't have said so, but what I did think amounted to my own ecstatic identification: the voice had gone, the style was intact. He still had a way!

3. Roland Barthes, *The Pleasure of the Text*, trans. Richard Miller (New York: Hill and Wang, 1975), 10.

PART II

SECOND TIMES

1. *SANSHO THE BAILIFF* (1954)

WITH CRITERION'S just-released digitization, our experience of *Sansho the Bailiff* has been split in two: there, in an evergreen jewel box, lies the precious *Sansho*-object in its best possible state; it has become a definitive edition, the Platonic idea of itself. But here, in our memories, lies the *Sansho*-aura, inseparable from the romance of reading *Cahiers du cinéma* and the thrill of watching scratched, dirty prints in run-down theaters at inconvenient hours. Once the same thing, object and aura are now estranged. The *Sansho*-object now looks harsh and unnatural in its digitized perfection, coolly removed from the past we shared with it. Not that this newly won hauteur does it much good; though relieved of myriad small defects, it has lost its grandeur (even literally: *Sansho* will never be larger than our TV screen); and in becoming immortal, it no longer bears life's vital signs. Meanwhile, the *Sansho*-aura submits to a fatal blow of its own; severed from organic contact with its object, it wilts into sentimental regret for a mere patina. If the Criterion *Sansho* keeps becoming a film we don't quite remember having seen, what we *do* remember of past viewings now strikes us as a dim prophecy that, being fulfilled, deserves to be swept away in the DVD revolution, along with the grime enshrouding the images and the grease sizzling on the soundtrack. Under these circumstances, it is almost certain that, by the year 2032, stalwarts of the old-time cinephilia will gather en masse to watch the facsimile of a deteriorating print of *Sansho the Bailiff*, complete with trashed images, the old grill cooking up a storm, and subtitling too butch to translate more than one phrase in ten. Admittedly, the congregants will worship in bad faith, as at a black mass, for in their hearts they will know that the true *Sansho*, the *Sansho* of which they sit adoring an effigy, abides in the evergreen shrine. Whence, if it could speak, it might boast with perfect honesty, "You know, I haven't aged in twenty-five years!" But there will be another irrefutable truth uttered when, at the end of the showing, one old man says to another: "now *that* was a pristine transfer!"

■ ■ ■

Sansho became famous for two things: one was its fable of redemption, of human dignity affirmed under the inhuman, albeit man-made, conditions of slavery and prostitution.[1] The other was its director's mise-en-scène, the spectacle of formal mastery that appeared in every composition, long take, and crane shot; this spectacle may have been called "subtle," "quiet," "tender," and "musical," but such terms were only an acceptable way to take the edge off an assertion of aesthetic will as aggressive as Hitchcock's. That the mythic fable and the famous manner are quite different things, the Criterion *Sansho* allows us to recognize as never before. For though Sansho's material deterioration obviously spared the fable, whose plot, characters, and themes survived intact in even the worst of prints, it did considerably dim the spectacle of Mizoguchi's style; with each new scratch, every fresh patch of obscurity, his framing lost some precision, his editing surrendered a bit of finesse. Though his main forms (the pictorialism, the long take, the crane shot) still loomed in the overall twilight, they were less seen than verified as trademarks. No longer able to command a response that would match its rigor, Mizoguchi's style circulated with *Sansho*'s bad prints as little more than mystique. We continued to parrot the *Cahiers* critics in pronouncing it "pitch-perfect," "beautiful," "elegant," and so forth, but the increasing vagueness of such descriptors only sealed the arcanum. In its degraded condition, the style became indistinguishable from the fable, an aesthetic variant on its humanist theme. *Sansho* appeared to bear its dull, spotted, scarred complexion with the same poignant dignity as that with which characters in the film endured face-branding, maiming, and prostitution; the stylistic feats resembled the human triumphs in being subdued and qualified, ultimately uncertain.

But if *Sansho*'s material deterioration had left its style rather literally in the dust, its material restoration now—quite usefully—throws its humanism in the shade. Unaltered, the fable plainly bears its historical date, the date of other post-war parables of man's "essential humanity" such as *Rashomon* (1950), *The Seventh Seal* (1956), or *Umberto D* (1951). The decorous understatedness extolled at Venice in 1954, in Paris in 1960, and in New York in 1969 (when I first saw *Sansho*), now seems the high-end wrapping on a forthright message movie. By contrast, the mise-en-scène, in being refreshed and hence defamiliarized, can never have enjoyed a fiercer power of address even in 1954 (when the fable, too, was new). There is no longer any danger that Mizoguchi's style will be subsumed to his fable, or his cinema to his humanism. In its superlative new rawness, the Criterion *Sansho* lets us grasp that style in its (cold, violent, ironic, creepy, "fascinating") *distance* from the humanist messages also being expressed in the film. Now that *Sansho* can be properly seen, we may not quite like what we see. For all its obvious beauties, something about it is hard on the eyes.

Can it be a mere coincidence that Criterion allows us, by pressing a single button on our remote, to replace this rejuvenated *Sansho* with a superannuated one as old as Heian Japan? In the exchange, the exigent images that have been cleaned of their dirt are once more covered up, this time in the anemic banality of Jeffrey Angles's commentary. Though bonded to the visuals like a lamination, this commentary has utterly nothing to say about them. It is too busy delivering a survey of tourist-grade Nipponiana: Noh, kabuki, gagaku, charcoal drawings, woodblock prints—everything from the front matter of a guide to Old Japan is called into service here, minus the section on lacquerware. Should this tactic be insufficient to distract our attention, Angles has another: he offers us a variorum of the Sansho legend, complete with all the episodes Mizoguchi left out or didn't know about. Of this commentary that, instead of commenting on the visuals, merely annotates them to death, the effective mission is clear: to rescind the restoration. Angles does more than not see the film; he unsees it.

But it would have been more honest to ignore the visuals entirely than to construct a pseudo-visuality in their place, as Angles also does. On the film's opening composition, a tree crossing the frame on the diagonal, he has this to say: "the use of space is reminiscent of pre-modern Japanese scroll paintings and woodblock prints that activate the foreground with some sort of dramatic movement." And on the final crane shot, this: "Critics have praised this shot of sea and sky as exquisitely Japanese, much like the dramatic landscapes we often see in sumi-e ink paintings." It is symptomatic of the edition's antivisual bias that it reprints Mori Ogai's 1915 source story as a bonus booklet—for the benefit of the variorum presumably—while it evinces no interest in reproducing even one ink painting or woodblock print that might make such points genuinely visual ones, instead of inert factoids. What Jacques Rivette observed in 1958 still holds for this misconceived Japanization of *Sansho*: "It may be that [Mizoguchi's] films owe something to the spirit of Noh or Kabuki, but then who is to teach us the meaning of those traditions?" And who, one might add, is to teach us why they are resorted to here, or how they are refashioned to fit the autonomous forms of cinema, an art unknown in premodern Japan and hardly reducible to its horizons? Who is to teach us that, in 1954, Mizoguchi's reminiscences of premodern tradition are necessarily signs of a chosen *relation* to tradition, of a rhetoric of traditionalism that places him in an ideological and not just a cultural field? But perhaps it is simplest to say that, at the end of this commentary's long night, all of *Sansho* remains to be seen.

■ ■ ■

What might there be to see? Always incipient in Mizoguchi's beautiful images and magisterial camera movements is a spectacle of the unwatchable. Ordinarily in *Sansho*, this unwatchable is merely intimated, as a sight we are being spared; cuts elide the face-brandings, and a crane shot averts us from the final tête-à-tête of mother and son (which, in its overwhelming emotional appeal, may be thought to pose its own threat to civilization). The Unwatchable has been less obstructed, no doubt, than decanted into cinematic form: the cuts are themselves rather violent, and the crane shot annihilates the human world more effectively than the vicious tsunami that we learn had swept over the same shore not long before. In one instance, however, Mizoguchi abandons even this much discretion. I have in mind an astonishing tracking shot—strictly, two shots fluently seamed together—in the chapter here called "Petition." Watch it with me.

Zushio, having escaped from Sansho's compound, is hidden under the veranda of the Emperor's chief advisor at Kyoto; he bears a testimonial that, if accepted, would put him once again in the company of free men. When the official crosses the veranda, Zushio starts up from beneath like an apparition; he bawls out his petition with similar vehemence—it is his only chance. Amazingly, the official remains unfazed; escorted by myriad attendants, he strides the entire porch without a single glance at the supplicant. But Zushio, too, is resolute. The camera tracks him for almost a full half-minute, as he scrambles along the ground, one hand clutching the railing, the other waving his letter, to keep up with the entourage on the porch. The longer his demand for recognition goes unmet, the more visibly hysterical he becomes. I mean that precisely, for what is most unbearable in this Via Dolorosa is his freakishly gaping eyes, which seem to have lost their human bearings; the pupils can't find a focus; if they were arms, they would be flailing in free fall. In classic cinema, which knows only significant glances, these eyes are a scandal; they are as hard to meet as those of a bird, baby, or madman. Our own eyes, as if catching their disorder, flee the intently sustained sight of them to the corners of the screen.

One reason the episode stands out is that no later scene fulfills its implicit narrative promise; Zushio never receives a look of human recognition that, equivalently pronounced and prolonged, might be seen to reverse its absolute withholding here. Even Zushio's mother—who so proper to bestow that mirror look?—has become blind by their final meeting. But another reason is the specifically cinematic intensity of the shot; though smooth as silk, even with the seam, the moving camera is hardly unassuming; its very gliding obtrudes in the stark contrast with Zushio's sideward hobbling. And in putting itself in the scene thus, the camera makes it a very different scene, a scene that no longer takes place in the fable, but in a strange proto-postmodern corridor that puts the fable in direct communication with its cinematic narration. In this different scene, the horror is not that the official refuses Zushio's look, but that the camera, from the very height from which the official might have returned that look, bestows its own. It is the peculiar ocular exchange that *does* happen, not the banal one that fails, which is responsible for the weird, inhuman "expression" in Zushio's eyes.

Petition untaken ...

Camera and character gaze at one another in mutually aghast fascination. The camera sees the human abjection from which—up where character is down, fluid where he stumbles—it tacitly claims its exemption. Character in turn sees an inhuman machine whose unrelenting scrutiny proves no less barbarously objectifying than the official's cold shoulder. But the

. . . and eyes unmet.

implicit recoil of each on seeing the other is equally the insinuated *attraction* of both to their uncanny mirror image. After all, Zushio, figure of "the human," pops into view as though on a spring, repeating the same words and gestures like an overwound robot. Conversely, the mechanical camera's sheer bravura confirms that it shares with him at least one distinctively human requirement: it, too, wants to be looked at, recognized. If the new DVD edition divides our experience of *Sansho*, it also lets us see with admirable clarity how conflicted this experience always was.

NOTE

1. As is well known, this fable involves the break-up of an aristocratic Heian family. The father, a provincial governor, is exiled for his activism on behalf of the peasants; on the way to join him, his wife and two children are kidnapped; she is sold into prostitution, they into slavery. In the compound of Sansho, the titular "bailiff" (slave-driver), the father's humanitarian values are tested in both Anju, the daughter, who retains them, and her brother Zushio, who becomes Sansho's right-hand man. Anju sacrifices herself so that Zushio may escape. Rehabilitated as an imperial official, he frees Sansho's slaves; and after their liberation, he resigns to go in search of his mother, now halt and blind. The film ends with their reunion on the shore of Sado island—or almost: a final crane shot turns from them to look on the sea, the seaweed, and a seaweed gatherer.

2. *CRUISING* (1980)

"THE LEATHER SCENE of *Cruising* is simply a background for a murder mystery." Ever since the filming of *Cruising* was disrupted by New York gay protesters in 1979, William Friedkin has made this point so often that, in his commentary on *Cruising*'s new DVD edition, doubtless impatient to be done with it once for all, he gives it the self-evidence of tautology: "The background of the leather bars . . . is simply a unique background." But no amount of mantric repetition can change the fact that where *Cruising* is concerned, the leather scene, precisely for its "unique" aspect, is not, nor ever was, simply a background. On the contrary, without this background, Friedkin himself was not interested in the murder mystery. When he was first asked to adapt Gerald Walker's 1970 source novel, whose homosexuals were slender, wore bangs, and did not, biblically speaking, know their ass from their elbow, he took a bored pass. That was before, wearing nothing but a jockstrap, and (just in case) accompanied by an armed mafia escort in the same costume, he started venturing into the Mine Shaft to see for himself the lately developed gay sex scene there. What he witnessed was galvanizing; it persuaded him that the novel, reset in this new milieu, could work on screen. His nocturnal visits recur in the film itself, where they are now paid by the protagonist Steve Burns (Al Pacino), a straight undercover cop who must infiltrate New York's gay leather bars and clubs in pursuit of a Homo Killer. The correspondent tracking shots are what made *Cruising* thrilling in 1980; and even today, they remain unbanalizable.

It is easy to see why. Meandering through the darkness of bars whose patrons are as likely to be sucking dick as swilling beer—and where even that beer seems destined to be pissed out

Flyer protesting against the production of "Kruising."

on men expectantly sitting in bathtubs for the purpose—the shots cast an almost blinding illumination on a sexuality that had been so deep in shadow as to be, until now, cinematically invisible. From being barely able to suggest what two gay men did at home between sheets, Hollywood suddenly proceeds to grant us a full and accurate idea of what scores of them were doing at the Anvil in slings. Very little *cruising* takes place in these shots (and that little appears satisfactorily concluded in fantastically short compass); most of the men are already getting off. No sad, solitary longing here; instead, a superabundant spectacle, as crowded with bodies as a Bosch painting, of acts and pleasures. The protesters were surely right to claim that *Cruising* continues a long Hollywood tradition of equating the homosexual and the homicidal, but in its predecessors— most notably Hitchcock's *Rope* (1948) and *Strangers on a Train* (1951)—the homicidal was all we saw; even to let us see the "sexual" in the "homosexual" to *any* extent, let alone as copiously as Friedkin has done, is a territorial conquest worthy of Cortez. And James Contner's cinematography rises to the occasion, washing the frieze of leather men with an ethereal blue light— exquisite halo for the denim and hardware on them—so that they stand out from their nooks and crannies like gilded saints in so many side-chapels. The film is scored to terrific original music from The Germs, whose punk pulsations, like everything else here, are too insistent to be just background.

For all their manifest aesthetic enhancement, these shots also carry documentary power. To the brave new world being imaged, Friedkin brought the authenticating procedures of neo-realism, using actual locations and mixing non-professionals in

Gay neorealism.

with his actors. These extras, not merely culled from the scene, were filmed actually performing the acts suggested. "I didn't give any direction to the people in these scenes; I just asked them to do their thing and let me film it." Though it lacks pornography's explicitness, the film shares in pornography's Bazinian embrace of the "ontology of the photographic image." The real places aren't simply like these; these are those places; the men in the background aren't simply got up to resemble the men in the places; they are those men. Their nipple-play isn't just play—or to put it differently, it's just play, not the demanding "work" that it would be supposed to be for union extras. *Cruising*'s dioramas convince us that gay sex happens, and this, in a culture vitally concerned with destroying every trace of homosexual desire, is by no means a universally self-evident proposition. Arthur Bell, instigator of the protests, feared that *Cruising* might well "send gays running back to the closet," but this misunderstands the probative force of the film's near-pornography. It is much more likely to have sent closeted gays running to the clubs to confirm its verisimilitude. We had not previously seen anything remotely like this depiction on screen, and the happy historical moment that favored it—after Gay Liberation but before AIDS, when curious straight men like Friedkin (due precaution taken) could indulge their fascination with the scene—is unlikely to be repeated.

■ ■ ■

Friedkin grasps the originality of the scene quite as much as did Michel Foucault, who saw in these "laboratories of sexual experimentation," as he called the SM backrooms of New York and San Francisco, a reinvention of sex, where "the idea is to make use of every part of the body as a sexual instrument." Prominent in *Cruising*'s laboratories, certainly, is the anal caress, a fondness for which is attested both by the many red and navy blue handkerchiefs protruding from back pockets and, with less formality, by the abundance of bare asses on parade. No longer privatized, but proudly displayed, tattooed, hairy, even dirty, these backsides (like the background in toto) insist on coming to the fore of our attention. But this anal responsiveness strays not only to other parts of the body (the armpits to be sniffed, the nipples to be chewed or tugged), but also to the body as a whole. Sometimes, indeed, the plugging-in of sex organs seems almost incidental to what is more fundamentally an ecstatic, X-rated cuddle whose goal is to put every body in total erotic contact with every other.

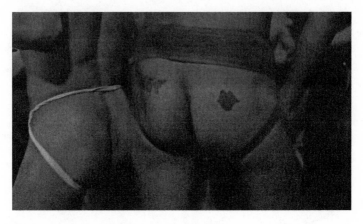

"Our assholes are revolutionary!"

Rather than anything more shocking, then, the sexiest practice depicted here, the one that comes nearest to incarnating full
body-readiness for each and every kind of embrace, is dancing.
The dance floor provides a kind of sexual antechamber, where
bodies, helpfully chloroformed with ethyl-soaked bandanas,
anticipate all manner of exposure, touching, grouping. That is
why the moment when Steve joins the dancing offers the most
satisfying "gaying" of his character possible, all the more inge-
nious in that, given that he's "the Pacino character," we would
never be allowed anything more explicit in any case. Unlike the
conventionally coupled gay ballroom-dancing in *Philadelphia*
(1993), Steve's dancing extends tangibility over his whole body,
so that whoever eventually touches that body—including his
girlfriend Nancy (Karen Allen)—and wherever it is touched—
including the least exceptionable spots—it has already wholly
been given over to the homosexual drift. That is the implied

meaning of the last shot, where Steve, his assignment over, shaves in front of a mirror; there, along with his haunted image, he discerns his Nancy behind him, wearing his leathers. Whom he has sex with will no longer prove much; his body has been desublimated, released from the organizational grip of sexual orientation. Is he now homosexual? All that seems certain is that he's no longer not. He's been queered.

■ ■ ■

The people and streets of Rome in *Open City* (1945) feel as if caught *sur le vif*, but the Good Priest, the Homosexual Villain, the Sacrificial Mother, the Youth of Tomorrow, and so on, are plainly myths recycled from nineteenth-century fiction via Hollywood. This dissonance between background and story (characters, situations, dialogue) is basic to the neorealist project, wherever it emerges; more, it is what the project exists to harmonize, promoting ideology to the status of the real while reducing the real to the ideological meanings it hosts. In *Cruising*, however, the neorealist enterprise is given this turn of the screw: the authenticity of the bar sequences sanctions the film's punitive wish to annihilate what it has glimpsed in them.

Follow the fist in this tightly compacted passage in the chapter called "Wanna Dance?" First we see a scene of fistfucking—extreme in any case, unprecedented on the Hollywood screen; there are shots of both partners, but our vision is mainly oriented by the man in the sling. We cut to a close-up of Steve watching from further back in the same perspective, his huge eyes as utterly engrossed as Friedkin's must have been

From fist-fucking . . .

. . . to fist-fighting.

on his first visit to the Mine Shaft, or, for that matter, as our own are likely to be at this very moment. Then, all of a sudden, a fist-fight breaks out between two patrons elsewhere in the club. The close-up of Steve looking marks—and masks—the transition between description and narrative: on one side of it, anonymous background figures who, however titillating, play no role in the unfolding story; on the other side, the arrival of a professional actor (Jay Acovone) playing a suspect, and, in his train, dramatic incident, enigma, psychology; the plot has visibly thickened. Under other circumstances, we might have observed that the verisimilitude—perhaps the reality—of the fisting has yielded to the almost comic implausibility—and unquestionable fictiveness—of a fist-fight in a gay club. But in this instance, any such perception is overwhelmed by the *force majeure* of a different sort of logic: the logic that would link, in any normal man, the prospect of being fisted to the speedy erection of his own dukes in defense. (The fighting words here: "Hey, asshole!")

Of course, Steve is not about to be fisted, nor is he involved in the fist-fight. He occupies a middle position between the two possibilities, not directly participating either in the "extreme sex" practiced by the gays, or in the violence that, albeit also here practiced by the gays, feels like its homophobic negation. But he's shown taking them both in, as part of the same exorbitant eyeful; through these wholly fascinated eyes, he internalizes the diptych as what will become his own psychomachia, and, ambiguously, his own narrative trajectory. It is important to note how merely *implicit* all this is, even mystified. "A gay man, whom I don't know, is using his fist on another gay man, whom I also don't know": this is the ambiguous Freudian dream that Steve entertains, and in it, his identification with both "victim" and "attacker" is buried alive in the self-ignorant relation of a fascination with the Other. Once we move from the background to a murder mystery starring Al Pacino, we say a decisive farewell to neorealism, and hello again to the celluloid closet, with all its strictly epistemological excitements. This closet gets reinstalled both in the story, as Steve's secret, "repressed" desire, so constantly under social censorship that we can barely be sure of its reality, and in the story's filming, as Friedkin's corresponding style of innuendo, ambiguity, elision, symbolism, and displacement. Having just seen gay sex unambiguously presented in the background, we reenter the old hopeful/fearful state of wondering whether it will ever materialize in the foreground, just as we once wondered, in *Rope*, whether the insinuated homosexuality of the protagonists would ever find denotation.

The abundance of evidence that homosexual desire no longer has to take this form seems only to have sharpened the vengeance with which it must now be repudiated. For Steve's Dream of the Fist replicates the film's own expedient fantasy, already in place, of an unidentified Homo Killer, a gay who murders gays in the very impetus of gay desire. In this fantasy, there is no gay sex unaccompanied by gay violence, as its intrinsic punitive counteraction: no butt-fucking without back-stabbing, no blow job without spurts of blood in place of cum; no polymorphous perversity without the body literally in pieces and floating in the Hudson. These are sides of the same coin, and the coin could hardly be in wider circulation. In the novel, there was only one murderer to be hunted, but in the film, he is ubiquitous, his identity having been pointedly disseminated across a number of different actors and characters: the killer in murder no. 1 is the victim in murder no. 2, while the actor who *plays* the victim in murder no. 1 is . . . The idea is to establish a symbolic circuit whereby every gay man, at varying degrees of separation, becomes his own assassin. But—here's the rub— the circuit is never quite closed; the overwhelmingly visible spectacle of gay male sex may be simply irresistible to any man who beholds it, and remain so even after its violent recloseting. In the final frenzy of his repression, Steve has probably killed his only gay friend; but given the sexual ambiguity of "murder" in the film, the homicide hardly de-homosexualizes him. The last shot insists that, however far he has removed himself from the scene, he will never remove its inscription from his pupils.

■ ■ ■

Faced with this coolly furious fantasy of gays loving/killing each other and—as we contract their homosexuality through our vulnerably wide-open eyes—turning each of us into a gay lover/killer, too, one is almost tempted to say that, if the AIDS epidemic hadn't happened, our culture would have had to invent it, as its exorbitant defense against the spill of gay sexual radicalism. Right after *Cruising*, in fact, the culture would proceed to do just that: invent AIDS, the "gay disease," Nature's rebuke to unnatural practices, God's way of weeding his garden, and all the rest. The film's banal paranoia would become horribly so. We must give the protestors this credit: before AIDS, they recognized the structure of AIDS panic.

Yet *Cruising* deserves a better queer analysis than they offered. To hear them go on, you'd have thought this "brutal arena" (as one of their flyers described it) was all Friedkin's sinister devising, and not the marvelous pleasure quarters it was for so many gay men, much less the momentous counter-cultural project described by Foucault or Guy Hocquenghem, who proclaimed: "Our assholes are revolutionary!" And let's be honest: would Martin Scorsese, with a mafia escort, have ever put on a jockstrap and descended into the Mine Shaft? Friedkin is openly as well as keenly curious about radical gay sexual practice, and, however much he may seek to protect himself or his viewers from its consequences, this curiosity visibly—ineffaceably—structures his film. The protesters' disingenuous, sex-phobic public relations have led the way to the present deplorable state of affairs, where all mainstream gay male representation aspires to the flaccid edification of an After-School Special, and the only gay men with a right to speak on the *New York Times* OpEd page are married with children! No doubt, *Cruising* lays down the same paranoid postulate as the classic thriller: *the homosexual will make us all homosexual.* (Guy to Bruno in *Strangers on a Train*: "Now you've got *me* acting guilty.") But the classic thriller also worked the paranoia through, via the death of the Homosexual, to the restored psychic health of its protagonist; in the end, it was as much of a marriage plot as *As You Like It.* But, signally failing to accomplish this achievement, *Cruising* instead shows that the paranoid defense against homosexual desire—albeit never before defended against more violently than here—can no longer be imagined with a successful outcome. This irresolution spoils the movie—spoils it, precisely, as a murder mystery. Responsible for the flaw, of course, is the background that refuses to stay in its designated marginal place. Having at long last seen this background, we can hardly avoid recognizing that we are *all* in it now, right up to our eyeballs.

3. *BERLIN ALEXANDERPLATZ* (1980)

BEFORE THE TREMENDOUS ORIGINALITY of Fassbinder's epochal film, the only honest response—still—is to gape and stammer. Small wonder that this admirable Criterion edition, albeit packed with supplements, lacks a commentary; the smooth-talking voice normally appointed to signify, with easy-going anecdotes and platitudinous background information, that a classic has been "classified"—sorted, digested, intellectually as well as digitally mastered—must have been struck dumb. Journalists have evinced a similar embarrassment around the film; though never allowed to be at a loss for words, they have channeled their facility elsewhere, into Wiki-dissertations on Alfred Döblin's homonymous 1927 source novel, or familiar evocations of Weimar Germany, with its brownshirts and cabarets. One may suspect that the diffidence is being carried a bit too far when Dave Kehr, in the *New York Times*, dismisses Fassbinder's film in favor of Phil Jutzi's mawkish ninety-minute 1931 adaptation;

or when Ian Buruma, in the *New York Review of Books*, reduces it to an occasion on which to plead for a new English translation of Döblin's Dos Passos pastiche, "brilliant and inventive enough to do justice to the text"! But even such aesthetic purblindness may be taken to prove the same point: *Berlin Alexanderplatz* is a film we don't yet know how to look at; in this respect, there might be something unpleasant and indeed repellent about the persistent demands it makes on our senses.

The inordinate length of the film (thirteen hour-long episodes with a two-hour epilogue) may suggest that we need the overviews provided by historical context or plot summary to guide us through it, but in fact nothing is less helpful than to superimpose upon the film's stylistic complexity—which is, after all, the thing to be looked at—the master narratives of History or the Novel. This is not because a historically situated narrative is lacking in *Berlin Alexanderplatz*—where, on the contrary, it takes the most legible generic form possible, that of melodrama—but because Fassbinder's cinematic style characteristically works at an off-angle to it. In virtually every image, there appears some perverse element—distracting, irrelevant, boringly emphatic—that refuses to serve the needs of the story, insists instead on leading, however inefficient or even counterproductive, a vehement life of its own. We need, then, less to "place" the film, than to grasp its capacity for unsettling *us*, and it is by paying attention to these often-annoying interferences that we best do so.

Let me begin with a frequent such interference, the garish neon light that flashes on and off in scene after scene (especially those in Franz's apartment, where the source of the pink radiance spasmodically bursting through the windows is never clarified). No doubt, this rather crude device produces a visual richness that remains broadly perceptible even on the small television screen for which *Berlin Alexanderplatz* was made. But it is hard not also to feel that its rapid, regular, mechanical rhythm overwhelms the subtler nuances, slower pace, and more varied actions of the human drama. Under different guises, such literally vibrant pulsation obtrudes nearly everywhere in the film. When we are not seeing it in a rotating fan or a teetering seesaw, fluttering leaves, flickering candles, or flashing lightning, then we are hearing it in sounds of ticking, dripping, buzzing, hammering, tweeting, or typing. Sometimes it is blatant, with each and every episode beginning under the aegis, visual and acoustic, of the chugging wheels of a train. And sometimes it is latent, a figure in the carpet: on the periphery of one scene, we may pick out a beggar's hand trembling up and down, up and down; in the background of another, we will discern a bird flying back and forth in its cage as if on a timer.

All this can hardly help getting on our nerves, rather as if, while we were trying to read or ruminate, we had developed a throbbing headache, or someone near us wouldn't stop mindlessly tapping his foot, or clicking a ballpoint. Much as, in episode 7, Franz becomes so disturbed by the ticking of a grandfather clock that he has to stop the pendulum, so we may often find ourselves wishing for an end to the stylistic tics that such ticking typifies. For underneath the full-bodied melodrama of the *Alexanderplatz*, Fassbinder seems to have set going a strange sort of metronome that makes us experience the film's length not as a richly novelistic accretion of characters and incidents, but as unalleviated duration, measured by a bare unmelodic beat without end. Detaching us from the narrative, this metronome, for all its quick drumming, is what makes the film feel so unnervingly slow. It dissolves the twists and turns of the plot into a suspense so sheer—because undefined (totally unlike Hitchcock's)—that we can hardly decide whether it heralds a deadly fate to come, or is itself that fate already at hand.

Merely annoying when it is extrinsic to the drama, the pulsing becomes more unsettling when we find it insinuated into the bodies, gestures, and voices of the *persons* of the drama, whom it seems, like an alien implant, to robotize from within. Our first shot of Franz introduces him, the very protagonist, less as a character with thoughts and feelings than as a *pace*. After a cursory head-on close-up, the shot does nothing but track him in profile as he walks—and walks and walks—along the prison courtyard, through accidents of light and shadow

Franz's long walk.

against a barely changing brick background. Over a minute long, it is an almost insanely extensive elaboration of a narrative action so minor that it is not even included in the source novel (whose first sentence already presupposes its accomplishment: "He stood in front of the Tegel Prison gate and was free now"). Franz's long, long walk is no journey to freedom, but rather, it already seems, the start of his subjugation by an enforced, inalterable, inhuman, and deadening repetition.

That stupefying prospect gets realized often enough in the *Alexanderplatz*, collapsing it into the kind of film in which "nothing happens." Betrayed by a fellow peddler, Franz goes on a monumental drinking binge during which he sets about emptying, one after another, crate after crate, an endless supply of identical beer bottles (episode 4). Later, after his girlfriend Mieze disappears, he sits in his apartment in front of a phonograph, playing his favorite song to death (episode 13). Even the ostensibly picaresque variety of jobs he takes in his sworn effort to go straight—selling tie-holders, pornography, the Nazi newspaper, shoelaces—proves balefully monotonous; these quasi-con jobs are not much different from the petty crime and pimping into which they prepare his inevitable relapse. In all his dubious touting, one is particularly struck by the declamatory quality of his speech, whose sing-song cadences give his utterances, from sales pitch to political rant to biblical quotation, the pumping rhythm of nursery rhymes—which he also sometimes declaims. It is as though, by embracing this rhythm, he were trying to comfort himself against the compulsive repetition of which it is, however, another index. (Similarly, during his drinking binge, he rocks himself back and forth in his bed.) Franz's drone finds an openly noxious counterpart in Reinhold's stutter, the impediment that the villain of the piece, for his part, desperately seeks to overcome with his machinations. That is what "plot" generally amounts to in *Berlin Alexanderplatz* (Franz going straight or getting together with Mieze, Reinhold changing girlfriends): a doomed attempt to mute the beat that is at the heart of everything here, destroying sense and soul alike.

■ ■ ■

The most disquieting vocal pulsation is Mieze's scream in episode 11 ("Two Surprises"). *Berlin Alexanderplatz* does not want for calamities, but this ululation troubles us more than any of them, Mieze's own murder included. And yet, in the very exorbitance of its intensity, it bears so vague a relation to the story that, though a supremely memorable moment, it is quite naturally forgotten in every précis. Its rather absurd narrative setting, in any case, may remind us more of *commedia all'italiana* than high tragedy. Smug, simple-minded Franz wishes to give Reinhold, incapable of staying with any woman for long, an object lesson in the value and art of loving relationships. He takes him home and hides him in his bed, where he may secretly observe the enviable picture of domestic happiness to unfold when Mieze returns. But Mieze returns with news Franz has not foreseen: she has met a young man—yes, she's in love with him! Ferocious with hurt and shame, Franz beats her and throws Reinhold, sheepishly emerging from the covers, out the door. And now, standing alone in the room, Mieze commences her great, harrowing aria: an uncontrollable oscillating shriek that, renewed with every breath she takes, perseveres to what feels like the span of an entire cantata. (It lasts a full minute, an unprecedented length in cinema.) Though the pink neon persists in flashing through the windows, and a birdcage swings violently overhead, there is for once no danger that the background interference will distract from the dramatic action, which simply consists in intensifying such interference exponentially, to the point that it no longer makes sense even to speak of action: the scream has arrested it altogether.

Only a short while before in the same scene, Mieze had wailed under Franz's brutal blows; he paid no attention to those cries, which hardly could be thought to require an explanation. But this scream terrifies him with a violence all the more dreadful in that it appears to him to be without cause. Huddled with Reinhold at the door and wide-eyed with fright, he demands, "Why are you screaming like that?" We too might pose that question. For Mieze has not screamed like that when Franz was beating her, nor will she scream like that even when Reinhold is about to kill her. We see Mieze in a static long shot in which, like Franz at the beginning, she shows only an inscrutable, soul-concealing profile. The remote visual treatment—Haneke *avant la lettre*—only further heightens the floating quality of our immediate aural intimacy with the scream itself. In the very genre of transparent feeling that is melodrama, Fassbinder has produced a blatant psychic intensity with no equally obvious corresponding meaning. The film's expressive high point is, in fact, a passionate *reticence*; in refusing to show its reasons, the scream multiplies the valences of its painful affectivity all over the place. At once under- and over-motivated, it becomes wildly

Mieze's scream.

enigmatic; because nothing directly accounts for it, everything obliquely might.

No doubt, the discovery of Reinhold in Franz's bed has set Mieze off. That Franz beat her may only prove that he can't bear losing her to another man, but that he beat her in front of Reinhold reveals a far more horrible state of affairs in which the real Couple is elsewhere, formed not by her and Franz, as even being battered by him she might still imagine, but by Franz and Reinhold, men who are using her in the no-longer-quite-un-conscious gesturing of their love for one another. Does Mieze believe she was about to be swapped between them, the latest piece of goods in the female-trading that, Reinhold has told her earlier, the friends practice together? Would she be then bewailing the structural pain, physical and psychic, suffered by all women in the gender/sex system that subordinates them not only to men, but also to the affective bond between them? Though Mieze has only been introduced in episode 8, her scream has been "waiting to happen" almost from the beginning, as if it were the unthrottled version of a ubiquitous female scream, one previously silenced or curtailed by Franz when it rose to the lips of Ida (about to be beaten to death), Minna (about to be raped) or Cilly (about to be abandoned).

But in giving voice to the long line of his cruelly abused women, Mieze's scream does something else besides. Agonized, it is also agonizing, inflicting no small part of the screamer's pain on whoever finds it, as we say, painful to hear. There is no way of reckoning how many men have sobbed in unmanned sympathy with Mieze, finding their own pain revealed in hers, but there is at least one: Franz himself. "You're screaming the whole house down," he declares, as if she were realizing his earlier fear that "the roofs might begin to swing and shake . . . slip down like sand." Mieze's scream has brought home to him the pain of his own psychosocial doom—a doom that had been sufficiently indicated to him by the prison, the delinquent milieu, his Zolian alcoholism, and finally his missing limb, but that he had been attempting to elude by, among other stratagems,

Franz's howl.

transposing it onto his women; in his violent or humiliating treatment of them, he could think of himself as the very agent of the pounding fate that cowed him in the rest of his social relations. But now, all of a sudden, he finds himself emitting antiphonal howls as he joins Mieze and the whole chorus of female figures behind her in that "shrieking of women" from which he once observed that a man liked to cut and run.

To halt his own sobbing, he attempts *to suffocate Mieze*, as if he could silence her as he did the clock. But in the process, he becomes clockwork himself: "Ich! Bring'! Dich! Um!" ("I'll kill you"), he intones while striking her, a stupid giant beating out his "Fee! Fie! Foe! Fum!" There is no escaping the unstoppable pressure of that pulse of which Mieze's scream offers not only an instance, but also a tragic recognition. The film ends with Franz unleashing a howl that, half manic laugh, half manic sob, is drawn out even longer than Mieze's. His face, already blocked by the birdcage, gets covered with a succession of end credits in what amounts to a brazen act of tagging: "This image belongs to Rainer Werner Fassbinder's *Berlin Alexanderplatz*." If a deathly pulsation is at work in Franz's world, then what has been meant by it, and what has been unmeant, is finally epitomized as the film's own style, with its maddening flicker of impediments. In the presence of this unsparing style, it is no wonder, if we are not, like Franz, to howl back, that we still shrink from taking its measure.

4. *BONNIE* AND *PIERROT*

A YOUNG CINEPHILE I know sat me down with him to watch two new DVD releases: *Bonnie and Clyde* (1967) and *Pierrot le fou* (1965). As he'd apprised me, the films were curiously related. Not only had the writers of *Bonnie*, David Newman and Robert Benton, set out to emulate the sensibility of French New Wave films; their screenplay proved so congenial to the sources of its inspiration that an admiring François Truffaut passed it on to an amenable Jean-Luc Godard, who entered negotiations to film it. These of course weren't successful, but when Newman and Benton later mused—sometimes with Godard himself—on what, as they put it, "*Bonnie and Clyde* might have been had he directed it," they imagined it would have been "not unlike *Pierrot le fou*," Godard's film about another couple on the run made only a year after the *Bonnie* deal fell through. Such information, like the ebullient young man who imparted it, charmed me considerably: could the proposed double feature fail to stimulate? For all our difference of age and sensibility, I too was a cinephile, and because of that same difference, I had confidence in us as a team; once we had warmed up with the child's play of finding Godard's example in *Bonnie*, we would easily advance to the trickier fun of spotting traces of *Bonnie*'s influence on *Pierrot*, a film that preceded it by two years. And then, who knew?

But somehow, for so suggestive a pairing, we weren't after all a good pair. To begin with, my companion, though a mere fledgling, displayed a near-perfect command of *Bonnie*, not only its every scene and image, but even its making, marketing, and critical reception; and he expatiated on everything from the oral sex to Pauline Kael with the same stultifying effect on me as the self-adoring infomercials that Warner Bros., calling them "documentaries," had put on a separate disc. Without question, *Bonnie* was still all he remembered from the last and only time he saw it, but that very fact reduced my own viewing of it to no *more* than he remembered; I assented to his every point, engaged with none. The awkwardness between us only increased when we moved on to *Pierrot*. For now, continuing to pervert the conversational obligation to "take turns," but in the opposite way, he fell into a sort of abashed silence, which he maintained unbroken throughout the film's most extraordinary moments; despite his boast to have first caught *Pierrot* at a small *cinéma d'essai* in the Latin Quarter, I began to wonder whether he had *ever* seen this film. It was, in any case, impossible to doubt that he was deferentially waiting for *me* to take the lead here, as he had just done with *Bonnie*. But I couldn't, being rather in need of some assistance myself; and if I had nothing to add to his garrulity before, I had nothing to put forward now in our deadeningly silent home theater.

As the young man was none other than myself, or rather the earlier self that I had been when I saw these films in the 1960s, it was troubling that he should have turned out to be so unsatisfactory. As Brice Parain told Anna Karina in *My Life to Live* (1962), "When you're twenty, you don't know . . . To be completely at one with what you love, you need maturity." This had been a convenient assumption as much for the young man whom it first allowed to watch art films in total incomprehension as for his middle-aged successor whom it subsequently authorized to find consolation for grizzled hair in a well-judging head. But this time around, things had fallen out to the exact contrary: my callow youth proved surprisingly adequate to the task of understanding *Bonnie*, whereas my wise ripeness kept me gaga when it came to getting *Pierrot*. Had I waited forty years to learn that, in the first case, I *did* know at twenty, and that, in the second, I would *never* know? By virtue of being either too good or too faulty, my memory had cruelly stripped both films of depth. With *Bonnie*, it turned up little more than the rote memorization of a student good at cramming; and with *Pierrot*, it had sagged into out-and-out amnesia, the lapse of a dotard who was now forgetting his keys, his glasses, everything. Nothing could have been less Proustian than this strange commemorative experience that, in its very flatness, didn't feel like "experience" at all; instead, it had deprived me of a sense of my own depth along with the films'. Crowded out between two forms of mental superficiality—all-knowing adolescence and mindless senility—I had lost the very possibility of the just-right subjectivity (psychologically deep, aesthetically confirmed, erotically complete) that, under the name of maturity, Parain had promised me.

■ ■ ■

My failure to see in *Bonnie* anything I hadn't seen in 1967 may be recast in less personal terms, as an effect of the film's own antivisual bias. This might seem a preposterous claim to make about a Hollywood movie that devotes obvious effort to being easy on the eyes: the good looks of Faye Dunaway and Warren Beatty, the 1930s costumes and locations, Arthur Penn's theatrical framings—these things have been plainly designed to procure us immediate visual pleasure, and they do. But such pleasure is "obvious" in the root sense as well: it is *in the way*, at once obstructive and preemptive. If we are instantly gratified in remarking *Bonnie*'s many notable "sights," that is because (albeit more or less unconsciously) we instantly *recognize* them; hence, no sooner do we lay eyes on them than we essentially stop seeing them. Our pleasure is a sort of relief at being spared the strain, the intensity, the exorbitance inherent in visual excitation, and at finding that excitation pacified under the sedation of the déjà vu. *Bonnie* is packed solid, so to speak, with familiar icons, from pictures of FDR to Philip Morris ads; and the better to make its images always-already reminiscent, it frequently resorts to "antiquing" techniques, introducing its protagonists in black-and-white snapshots, or shooting Bonnie's family reunion through hazy window screen.

During one of the infomercials, Morgan Fairchild says of the faces in that reunion: "they look just like they're right out of a *Grapes of Wrath* 1932 photograph." This is pure eye-wash, but as such it is telling: what matters is that the déjà vu be *easily* recognized, not accurately; and indeed, the more vaguely we remember the icons of Grant Wood, Norman Rockwell, Dorothea Lange, Walker Evans, John Ford, or John Steinbeck, the

Déjà vu aesthetics I.

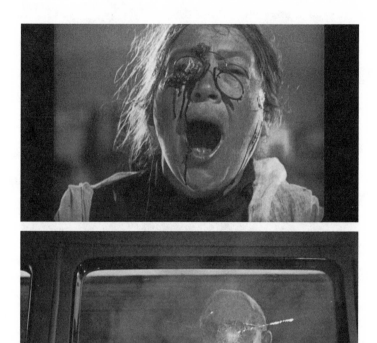

Déjà vu aesthetics II.

more effectively the film drains from them the blood to pump life into its phantom replications. Everything looks "just like it's right out of" something we can't quite name, but it would decidedly spoil the effect if an improved memory were to recall that Bonnie's trend-setting beret has been lifted from Peggy Cummins in *Gun Crazy* (1949), or that what is perhaps the film's most admired image—of a bank clerk seen through a car window as Clyde is shooting him—is modeled on an image from *Potemkin* (1925).

As if to forestall some such suggestion that *Bonnie* were anything other than original, its collaborators concur in recalling a magical, propitious creativity. Here is the costume designer Theadora van Runkle on her inspiration: "the minute I read the first page [of the script] . . . I knew, I saw every-thing." And here is Dunaway on the result: "The minute I saw it, I knew this was right." We too enjoy this amazing speed and range of vision in our humble capacity as *Bonnie*'s spectators: having seen everything before, we see it again "at once" and in its obvious "rightness."

There is a single exception to the film's practice of visual habituation, only one thing that induces rapid movement in our icon-glazed eyes. This is Dede Allen's editing, whose irregular hiccups keep breaking the spell of Penn's immobilizing tableaus and silhouettes with, at least for a while, some of the recklessly destructive energy of the protagonists themselves. Allen's work was called iconoclastic and it literally remains so, shattering the images by breaking up the tranquil, predictable flow required for their coalescence. This New Wave style of editing would soon become no more French than the baguettes on which, during the same period of assimilation, we were learning to make turkey sandwiches; but in *Bonnie*, at least, the contradiction it introduces is so serious as to require a full-on spectacle of resolution. In the same moment that the narrative tension comes to catharsis with Bonnie and Clyde's violent death, the formal antagonism is being resolved in the film's most spectacular—and transmissible—stylistic innovation: violence in slow motion. This device, which moralizing critics once censured for reveling in the violence, in fact does the very opposite; it abandons the iconoclasm of montage for a smoother, almost velvety transition between images, images that, in pointed contrast to the blood being splattered in them, now seem to be congealing. Bonnie is ridden with bleeding holes while *Bonnie* lyrically affirms its visual consolidation. The quick, staccato rhythm now belongs only to the feds' guns as the film's own pace is slowed down into a picture-pretty memento of what it had been; the editing has got "antiqued" along with everything else. *Bonnie*'s innovation thus consummates the film's very retro-ness, as a movie made in full anticipation of the nostalgia that it might one day occasion and is actually occasioning from the start. "You will remember *Bonnie and Clyde*," the film seems to be predicting with every image, "and you will remember *how good it used to look*." But the course of time, instead of making this prophecy easier to fulfill, has made it simply impossible: "I can't; I remembered that already."

■ ■ ■

Pierrot's heroine, called Marianne Renoir (Anna Karina), is shown standing next to a postcard of a Jean Renoir portrait, her hair done up in a somewhat similar way. But we can't possibly think that this image has just stepped out of the Renoir painting; precisely in being *comparable* to the latter, it has lost the possibility of seeming *like* it. While the mystificatory tact of allusion made Bonnie look "right" in her beret, the bald precision of reference gives this conjecturally Renoiresque image of Marianne a sharply defined inconsistency. Moreover, though many are the tricks and devices of Godard's style, they all work at the single task of making every cinematic image likewise incongruous, dissonant. A Godard image may be at odds with the music accompanying it, the dialogue spoken in it, or the quotation delivered over it; may run contrary to how narrative function and cinematic convention lead us to envision it; may diverge from the other images that it precedes, follows, includes, or imitates; may do all these things at once. But it is always a strikingly ill-suited thing. And this overall style of mismatching is itself strikingly ill suited to our attention, which, with equal abruptness, it at once summons and refuses to sustain.

By some reckonings, *Pierrot* marks the moment where Godard "goes bad," and by others, where his style, whose distinctive features had emerged long before, achieves its first fully rigorous statement. It is both these things because Godard here no

Two Renoirs.

longer puts up much resistance to the corrosive implications of this style for what had been his favorite subject (the romantic couple) and his favorite set of forms (the Hollywood genres). Adorable in *Breathless* (1959), irresistible in *A Woman Is a Woman* (1961), "fatal" in *Contempt* (1963), the couple in *Pierrot* enjoys only the charm of the fading. A mundane way of putting Godard's famous claim that his Marianne and Ferdinand (Jean-Paul Belmondo) are "the last romantic couple" is to say that they are, from the very beginning, at the end of the line, where all their effort to *be* the romantic couple is balked or unproductive. They are never seen even to accomplish the copulation that is the couple's crown in *Bonnie*, much less to hold together on any ideal or spiritual plane. More tiresome than poignant, their failing condition persists until the day they die—and even then, unlike every other couple on the run, they don't die together. *Pierrot's* couple runs not like *Bonnie's*, to its apotheosis in legend, but only like a stocking, as part of its own unraveling. The story of course unravels with it, on the application of the same inconsistency principle. "I didn't pre-think it," Godard rather proudly told *Cahiers du cinéma*; "it was a completely spontaneous film," written, edited, mixed as he went along. We don't doubt his sincerity here, but neither do we appreciate the film's perfunctory and confusing narrative construction. Released from the thrall of Couple and Genre, *Pierrot* deprives us of conventional mnemonics to remember it by.

Yet the profoundly unmemorable freshness of *Pierrot* derives from more than just these deficiencies of content and form. Consider what Samuel Fuller, playing himself, says early on when Ferdinand asks him just what exactly cinema is:

"A film is like a battleground. It's Love. Hate. Action. Violence. Death. In one word, emotions." Those who quote this one word as gospel must have, like me, forgotten ever seeing *Pierrot*, for who that had remembered could think of "emotions" as anything but bad subtitling for a film that doesn't depict or induce any? Love, hate? Between this nonchalant couple, they are hard to find, still harder to feel. Violence, death? But these are hardly emotions, and in any case are too factitiously presented, with blood by Mondrian, to grip us; the protagonists themselves seem unfazed by the corpses dropped their way. In any case, the inscrutable Fuller, his eyes covered in dark glasses, has made the very driest case for emotions, and the burp-like brevity of even Ferdinand's response—"ah!"—seems to equate understanding with dismissal. All we see in either man is a nonplussed surface that may or may not be concealing anything deeper down. Not by chance does the only thing on which Marianne and Ferdinand ever agree prove to be this expressionless quality of the visual image, which, as they both separately claim, never reveals anything about a subject's interiority, even that it exists. In this, unlike Fuller on emotions, they are truly speaking for *Pierrot*'s maker. Devoid of expression, of desire and the affect around it, Godard's images deny us any hospitable site from which we might *imagine* them— deepen them with desire or affect of our own. They put us in the depressive position of "having eyes bigger than our stomachs," of having to keep confronting what, libidinally speaking, we can't take in. Existing only in an imaginary *sostenuto* that Godard never gives, emotion is precisely what his cinema will not let us visualize.

Take, for example, from chapter 17, the long, slow pan that begins following Ferdinand as he walks desultorily along the railway tracks. We hear a train whistle; he sits down between the rails. He buttons his jacket, looks up, then down. We hear another, longer whistle. The train approaches, Ferdinand gets off the tracks; it passes and he walks on. On the basis of this shot, Criterion has called chapter 17 "Despair." But this is only more bad subtitling, willfully reading "into" the shot so as to restore the melodramatic emotionality that everything about it is rendering moot. It is equally false to say, as does Peter Whitehead in the screenplay's English translation, that Ferdinand "staggers up" "at the last minute" and "just escapes" being hit by the train. Much as the equanimity with which Ferdinand installs himself on the tracks indicates less despair than a lightly worn apathy, so the unpanicked ease with which he gets up and off them suggests that his putative suicide attempt is no more than an idle game he perhaps already knows how to play. His disconsolate words ("ah, what a terrible five o'clock in the afternoon! The blood, I don't want to see it") echo lines from a famous elegy by García Lorca for Ignacio Sanchez Mejías, a bullfighter fatally gored in the ring; but the *corrida* is a self-canceling signifier: along with the ennobled ghost of Mejías, Godard's reference calls up Disney's silly cartoon bull, also called Ferdinand and remarkable for sitting down. At all events, the borrowed verses submit to the same erratic treatment as any other citation in Godard, first repeated, then inverted, finally cut off in medias res—right after the "ah," in fact, as if the plug had been pulled on the audio—death by technological failure—or as if we were again hearing Ferdinand's curtly non-absorptive response to Fuller on emotions.

From the early silents on, fiction cinema has loved elaborating the fearful danger of being run over by a train; but Godard seems to evoke this classic thrilling situation only to have us observe his methodically cool rendering of it. He avoids the usual sympathetic close-ups and suspenseful cross-cutting; he even, for once in *Pierrot*, abates the assault of primary colors, as if unwilling to risk, in such a context, hitchhiking on their visual intensity. In the most perverse touch of all, he entrusts the process of glaciation to a long crane shot, the very shot that he has inherited from Mizoguchi and Hitchcock as the privileged vessel of sustained emotion. Now, no longer justifying its movement in the character's literal and emotional rush, which in any case is lacking here, the camera moves as desultorily as does Ferdinand. There could hardly be a blunter negation of the cinema of emotions, or a more thorough abolition of its sense of dramatic event. If Ferdinand had died here, would much feel changed? His corpse would only lie there in its pool of red paint like the others before it; at best it might prompt us to repeat what would have become his last word: that very unsatisfactory "ah." What would happen, in other words, is not very different from what does happen at the end of *Pierrot*, when Ferdinand wants to blow himself up, changes his mind, but then blows up anyway: "I see" is all the response we can muster.

But suppose that Godard were imaging here emotion of a different sort from the imaginary emotions of a story. I have just said that the absence of parallel montage in the treatment is a refusal to develop the emotion—call it "a fear of death"—conventionally implied in the fictional situation; but it may be doing something else besides. Think how much André Bazin admired the shot in

Perils of *Pierrot*.

Where No Vultures Fly (1951) where a child who has picked up a lion cub is shown in the same frame with, in one direction, the lioness in search of that cub and, in the other, the parents in search of that child. This single frame, Bazin affirms, "in which trickery is out of the question," puts the characters in a real situation and gives the story the authenticity of a real event; as such, it "carries us at once to the heights of cinematographic emotion." In Godard's shot, likewise "without trickery," one sees that there must have been a possibility—surely minimized, but nonetheless irremovably genuine—that Belmondo would be run over by the train. Godard no doubt trusted his star, whose athleticism is on triumphant display throughout *Pierrot*, to decamp on cue, but it is startling to imagine—no, *not* to imagine, that is the point, but simply to *see*—the deadly, vital risk that must have been taken. Yet whereas, for Bazin, such "cinematic emotion" serves to legitimate and even magnify the imaginary narrative emotions by grounding them in bona fide reality, in Godard here, the cinematic emotion neither reinforces ordinary emotion, nor feels anything like it. For if the film-*story* always unfolds in the present tense, the film-*making*, by the time we see any of it, is always over; *Pierrot*'s shot simultaneously informs us that, while Ferdinand may be in danger, Belmondo can only *have been* so. What the strange and disorienting absence of intensity in his performance here makes us confront is the dispiriting weirdness of cinematic emotion. At this moment of real danger, we are at last in the presence of some vestige of "real emotion," but it is as if we have—as we always will—come upon it too late to appropriate it, to feel *with* it. No wonder *Pierrot* is unmemorable: how can we remember an emotion about which we know nothing but that it must have taken place?

5. *ROCCO AND HIS BROTHERS* (1960)

WHY THIS new Masters of Cinema (MOC) edition of Luchino Visconti's *Rocco and His Brothers* was undertaken—what necessity or desire it was intended to meet—an oracle alone could tell us. The image, though anamorphically well-proportioned, is hardly different from the 2003 Medusa edition, and even most of MOC's "new, improved" subtitles come from that edition. When these *are* new—and turn, say, a character's "weakness" for boxers into his "generosity" toward them, or send us looking for an invisible "picture" of San Rocco while the statue of him sits in plain view—their prudery and ignorance only resume *Rocco*'s dismal history of censorship. Perhaps not everything about the original should be restored, and certainly not, in *Rocco*'s case, the superannuated conceptual framing that MOC has also salvaged for the accompanying booklet. The latter consists—exclusively—of texts written around the time of *Rocco*'s release by Visconti and his intellectual champion and fellow party member Guido Aristarco. These enlist *Rocco* under the banner of political and artistic traditions then regarded as progressive. Visconti invokes Gramsci's "Notes on the Southern Question," to which *Rocco* would give narrative form, while Aristarco sees the film as continuing not only the left-leaning neo-realism of post-war Italian cinema, but also the explicitly proto-Marxist "critical realism" that Georg Lukács finds in the nineteenth-century European novel.

In 1960, it perhaps required such a pedigree to persuade the Italian cultural Left of *Rocco*'s merit. To many of its first spectators, Visconti's great work seemed morbidly afflicted with melancholy, and this condition had to be neutralized, as by an antitoxin, with vigorous insistence on the film's "optimism of the will" (Visconti) and "presentiment of a great transformation to come" (Aristarco), which, appearances to the contrary, made it acceptably inspirational. But such affirmation, disingenuous even in *Rocco*'s original marketing, becomes sheer mystification when reintroduced as the default setting for viewing *Rocco* now. The film's political value today might be said to lie, if anywhere, in the extreme formal clarity with which its melancholy prevents its Marxian dialectic from being more than notional. Unrecognized and even ruled out by Visconti's dutifully hopeful script, this melancholy survives in those appearances to the contrary which are, precisely, the images themselves.

If we started from these images rather than the script, we would see at once, for instance, that *Rocco* is simply too beautiful to be a neorealist film. No doubt, the story—of a transplanted southern Italian family in Milan—takes place in that poor and lowly social realm which is neorealist territory par excellence; in

addition, it deploys practically the whole set of neorealist stereotypes from the virtuous man and the chthonic mother to
the creepy homosexual and the child redeemer—only the dog is
absent. But the images egregiously violate neorealism's two chief
visual canons: ordinary-looking people and natural lighting.
Rocco's beauty—distracting indeed—pulls us away from both
conventions. To begin with the first of these, no one can pretend
for a moment that Rocco Parondi, country boy and world-class
boxer, looks like anything but the exquisitely handsome movie
star who plays him, Alain Delon; or that his uncouth brothers
Simone, Vincenzo, and Ciro (Renato Salvatore, Spiros Focás,
and Max Cartier) do not share with this champion the title of
Best-Looking Male Ensemble in the All-European Cinema.
What's more, the Parondi beauty is so widely mirrored throughout the film's large population of boxers, soldiers, workers, and
other assorted male extras, that, in a quite un-Marxist sense, all
men truly do seem like brothers: the millennial class divisions
of plain and handsome have been overcome at last, and muscles
and well-built frames, so unjustly distributed everywhere else,
are here the common property of all.

Curiously, this extraordinary male beauty never sees much
narrative service, even in the romance plots. In Visconti's earlier *Ossessione* (1943), the mere sight of Massimo Girotti with
an open collar impelled Clara Calamai to a fatefully infatuated
double take. Here Nadia (Annie Girardot) first regards Rocco's
fine features and form with perfect nonchalance; what she falls
for—and then only a couple of years later—is the mystique of
his innocence. And while the sight of Simone in the shower
probably does excite his promoter Morini (Roger Hanin), who

The lineup of beauty: Rocco, Simone . . .

calls him a "young Apollo," the celluloid closet's usual operation makes this homosexual undercurrent so elliptical, obscure,
contradictory, and deniable that, if there is a story here, it is not
one the film is willing to come out with. With a homelier cast,

. . . Vincenzo, Ciro.

Rocco's story would not only require little alteration; it would also gain more plausibility. From a narrative standpoint, the Parondi brothers are beautiful for nothing, like garments too fine to wear.

Yet there is no inhibition of the film's tendency to show one or another of them, especially Rocco, posed in an appreciative close-up or long shot. Though their beauty does not motivate the story, the story is frequently managed so as to motivate that beauty's extraneous display. Vincenzo is dull-witted, Simone sluggish, Rocco dreamy, and Ciro serious: all torpefying traits that rationalize the loitering camera's predilection for an equally lingering image. The labor of these proletarians—obviously no beautifier—takes place off-screen. What they are most frequently shown doing is dressing or undressing; and as they put on their shoulder-hugging sweaters and tight jeans, or strip down to underwear and boxing trunks, they are attractively drowsy, numb, bewildered—so consistently absent-minded, in a word, that they seem like creatures under enchantment. Even pugilism, whose incessant agitation might be thought to shatter this enchantment

MOC booklet cover.

together with the *bel profilo* it shows to such advantage, comes under its spell: the boxers are sleepyheads. With "lead legs" and "slower than an ox," Simone must be frequently admonished to "wake up" in the ring; and Rocco, too, fights in a reverie, as if (to use his own metaphor) he were shadow-boxing in the mirror. Further, when he is shown doing just that, the resulting image is so powerfully iconic that MOC, oblivious to the Southern Question, has put it on the booklet cover.

This general narcolepsy—so different from the usual "determined" male hyperactivity in cinema—invests the brothers with the mystery, the erotic fascination, attending anyone we see in his sleep; it makes them at once completely remote from real contact and fully available to fantasy appropriation. It is crucial to *Rocco*'s somnolent beauty that the brothers also be unawakened in the sexual sense, or at least seem so on the visual plane. In the absence of any chemistry between two such living dolls as Focás and Claudia Cardinale, for instance, it is anyone's guess how Vincenzo gets Ginetta pregnant; and Franca (Alessandra Panaro), doling out kisses like after-school cookies, is more mother to Ciro than girlfriend. As for Rocco—who is literally called the Sleeping Beauty by the girls at the laundry where he is briefly employed—he remains celibate throughout the film. Even with Nadia, everything stays on the surface, charmingly unconsummated. One of Simone's stated reasons for raping Nadia is to give Rocco, forced to witness the outrage, a lesson in sex education: he will show Rocco what Nadia "is," "how she makes love"; and as he flings her panties at (or rather onto) Rocco's face, he shouts, "Kiss them if you have the courage; you can only make love with these."

The beauty of Rocco and his brothers, then, lies in their splendidly inert chrysalis, which, in signaling the "immaturity" of their sexuality, preserves it in an appealingly polyvalent state of indefinition. Though often classically feminine in its poses and accessories (Vincenzo wears a flower, Rocco his mother's sweaters), this larval beauty embodies not the culturally repellent catastrophe of men who have become women, but the culturally endearing idyll of men who are still boys. In the sleepy limbo of latency, all things seem possible, because none has submitted to the mangling limitations of social realization and rule. For whether tragic or merely tiresome, the mature forms of male sexuality in *Rocco* are not pretty: molestation at one end, dutiful conjugal procreation at the other, and furtive homosexuality hovering over the entire range. Beauty, on the contrary, consists in the film's provocatively odd suggestion, at once utopian and defeated, that these things are best held in abeyance, in a sort of natural unconscious chastity. Accordingly, it makes perfect sense that Simone, the only brother whose adult sexual state gets visualized (in the seriously ugly forms of whoring, rape, and hustling), should lose his looks in the process. His face becomes drawn, his figure puffy, and—worst of all given the film's aesthetic of repose—he gets the shakes.

■ ■ ■

Rocco's too-beautiful beauty cannot be ascribed solely to the photogeny, however considerable, of its dormant male protagonists. It is also owing to Giuseppe Rotunno's comparably breathtaking cinematography. *Rocco*'s great *tableaux vivants*, as classically structured in their way as Delon's face and Salvatore's torso are in theirs, give only the half of it. We might find similarly pictorial compositions in a neorealist work such as *Umberto D* (1952)—and with reason: its cinematographer Aldo Graziati not only worked for Visconti in *La terra trema* (1948) and *Senso* (1954), but also had Rotunno as his assistant for many years. Yet the artfulness of *Rocco*'s images is not discreetly obscured, as in De Sica, under naturalizing natural light; it is flaunted with all the synthetic luster, the artificial halo, common to the urban night and to classic black-and-white studio lighting.

I am especially struck by a certain glassiness that—unevenly, but insistently—overruns sections of the image, almost as if they had begun to freeze over, or were being laminated. This pervasive icing—here a spark or glimmer, there a more consistent sheen or glare—only partly results from vitreous surfaces (wet cement among them) reflecting the spots and arcs behind the camera or the numerous neon signs, light poles, headlights, lanterns, lamps, and candles in front of it. Not only do we see a lot of glass; we also often see through it, in the form of tram windows, car windshields, gym mirrors, display cases, and frosted doors. Rather than tactfully conceal its presence in the neorealist manner, the camera compulsively projects its lens into a world that often looks as if it has been put under a bell jar. On a dresser in the Parondi household, a bell jar in fact stands prominently displayed; covering a figurine of Rocco's patron saint and surrounded with votives, it gleams suggestively.

But there are other and better emblems of the film's *beau idéal*—namely, the glossy or glassed-over photographs that we see all over the place from Cerri's office to Morini's apartment

A world of glass.

to the Parondi household, where, for lack of separate rooms, each brother's turf is marked by his tract of pictures on the wall, and a large family portrait dominates the whole. Such ubiquity bespeaks less the characters' aggregate fanaticism than the overriding obsession of the film itself, which holds up these photographs as literally shining examples of the visual perfection that it seems keen or anxious—in any case, compelled—to attain. With its own manifest fondness for fixed frames and successive close-ups, for photographic lighting and glazed surfaces, *Rocco* is a film that seems as invested in looking like a studio photograph as it is in making the Parondi brothers pose for one.

Although indissolubly bonded, however, the two kinds of stillness—that of male latency and that of the photograph—by no means share the same implications. Latency, in making the

Rocco among pinups.

subject's development an open question, is all sweet promise and suspense. By contrast, the photograph, with its proof that the subject "has been" (Barthes), records both an eternal fixity and an absolute past; there will be no awakening or breaking out, and even the moment of its possibility has fled. The innumerable photographs *of* latency in the film thus at once preserve their subject and write its epitaph, transforming the fresh and untouched into the fetishized and untouchable. In them, the forward-looking time of the content so intimately collapses into the backward-looking time of the medium that latency appears as a sort of souvenir of itself. That is why these photographs are always objects of pathos, nostalgia, denial, melancholy; their scintillant skin glorifies the dead-and-gone no less than the bell jar that covers San Rocco's statuette in the

Parondi apartment or, for that matter, the glass tomb encasing his corpse in Venice.

■ ■ ■

And the film's own frames or photograms? Compared to photography, of course, film is much better suited for rendering vital signs; here, the image seems to move, and the human figures in it to live and breathe. Yet film also enjoys a variety of means to arrest the image flow, slow it down, or otherwise reveal it as a mere succession of photographs. Like any other motion picture, *Rocco* necessarily brings its still images to life, but if it thereby gives its slumbering male beauties the added charm of cinematic respiration, it also contrives to stifle the fairest of all in photography's eternal rest. Watch with me a shot that, never figuring in "political" readings of the film, and scarcely mentioned even in plot summaries, may be the film's most beautiful and is certainly its most shocking. I mean the prolonged, increasingly tight close-up of a recumbent Rocco that occurs in the middle of the film (at the end of the "Stolen Broach" chapter). Rocco and Simone have been lying on adjacent beds; Rocco has a message for Simone from Nadia: she is going away, destination withheld. When Simone hears this, the rage simmering in his voice belies the indifference professed by his words: "You know her, too? But what does she want with me? She's just another whore, who thinks she's a great lady. Let her go to hell! If I see her on the street again, I'll turn my head the other way. Tell her that, if you see her again, tell her I said that!" And then, as if he were rehearsing the street encounter with Rocco in Nadia's place, he turns away from him and goes to sleep. Throughout this conversation, the camera, instead of cutting, has simply traveled back and forth from one brother to the other, creating an odd continuity between them. But now it stays with Rocco, framing him in profile on his bed. He slowly turns his head toward us, and crooks an arm behind it, as if pensive. The camera gets closer and closer until Rocco's face fills—and threatens to overfill—the screen, which then fades to a new scene with the title "Rocco" written over it.

In narrative terms, the close-up seems almost ostentatiously futile. "As if pensive," I have written to make the best of it. But what has Rocco to think about, really? What motivates his brother's outburst is obvious straightaway: Simone is hurt and angry, insanely in love with Nadia, and already prepared to view Rocco as a rival. And if Rocco reflected on these things in *any* degree, let alone for as long as the shot goes on, he would not be so naive as to get involved with Nadia (in the very next scene!), or to be surprised by Simone's fury when the involvement is discovered. How can Rocco forget what this prolonged episode of thoughtfulness should have engraved on his mind so *memorably*?

But of course something else is going on, as becomes grippingly plain as soon as Rocco turns his face to the camera. He is not thinking at all. He is *letting himself be looked at*, offering his exquisite face and flesh to the camera with the thrillingly unqualified submissiveness of an odalisque. The resulting image offers a limit case of latency, an expectancy so heavily underscored, so ripe, that it seems on the verge of exploding into event. The languorous pose may remind us of Girodet's

Endymion, but not the assertion of axillary hair, which is so startling to see on Delon's glabrous white body that we almost feel we have witnessed a sudden sprout of pubes. More: while Delon may be simply looking at the camera, we know that what

Dying into the close-up.

is filling Rocco's vacant eyes off-screen is the sleeping figure of
Simone. Rocco in a daze, Simone in a doze: the two latencies,
proximate and opposed, intensify our sense of this moment as a
fatal coupling, a "Hitchcockian" encounter at once homoerotic
and transferential.

As if the calamity of this coupling were prophetically
impacted into Rocco's eyes, the shot, continuing on, transforms
the homoerotic image into a deathly one. The camera keeps
closing in on Delon's face, as if, in response to its overwhelming
appeal, it were going to kiss it, but—as happens with a kiss—the
visual pleasure gets spoiled the nearer we get. The sexy armpit
vanishes. The proportions of the face grow too large to sit com-
fortably, not to say classically, in the frame. We start to observe
such pores, wrinkles, and other minor imperfections on the skin
as to suggest the skull beneath. And the eyes are as fixed and

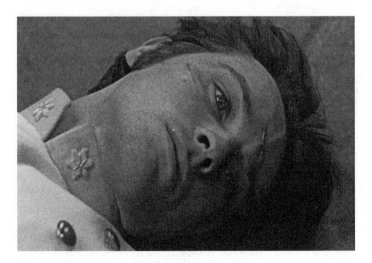

Dead.

motionless as in a freeze-frame; if they did not give a final blink to shake us out of this morbid perception, we would think they were glass eyes or a zombie's. The shot that first blooms as a living pin-up droops into almost a morgue slide. Rocco seems to be dying into a photograph of himself. (Would this be Delon's on-screen destiny too? A close variant on this mortuary image appears in *William Wilson*, Louis Malle's segment of *Spirits of the Dead* [1968], where Delon-Rocco's deathliness becomes Delon-Wilson's actual represented death.)

■ ■ ■

Later in the film, Rocco's superstitious mother Rosaria (Katina Paxinou) suspects that someone has put the evil eye on him; in the absence of any literal evidence to support this idea, it is tempting to suppose that the *malocchio* was cast in the very close-up we have just described, so heavily did the camera's gaze appear to weigh on its object. Soon enough, in any case, the close-up's implicit trajectory finds extravagant enactment in Rocco's story. In the film's great climax, Rocco and Simone are once again lying on a bed. But now the bed is shared, and the others have been shut out of the room. "I killed Nadia," Simone confesses, and Rocco, though screaming "No! No!" in disbelief, throws himself on him, vehemently sobbing and heaving. "Isn't that what you wanted?" Simone continues, and Rocco, though now screaming, "I know I'm guilty," holds him even tighter. Just before this exchange, as the brothers enter the bedroom, and Rocco violently slams the door, a small tinkling sound is heard, the noise of breaking glass.

But no, it is likely only the door key fallen to the ground, and it will, one infers, be put back in place, since after this melodramatic outpouring, Rocco reverts to his former celibacy with a vengeance. And the vengeance seems more than anything directed against himself: once pure promise, his state is now pure privation. He will serve out his youth alone, without brother or friend; in exile, not only from Lucania but from Italy too; and supporting himself through an activity—boxing—that he despises. This living death is perfectly captured in the still life that is our last on-screen view of him. Rocco ends up literally becoming a photograph—the cover image on a boxing magazine, of which numerous copies have been pinned up in a row at the newsvendor's. In these images, Delon could almost pass for a boxer at last; his face is now so gaunt that his delicate facial bones protrude as if out of joint; we might be looking at a series of x-rays. But more directly to the point of such neatly aligned images, we might also be looking at a piece of filmstrip, and a quite peculiar one at that. For the successive images are all identical; were such a strip to be projected, we would see only a freeze-frame, the ultimate negation of Bazinian "becoming" on film. We could hardly ask for a more explicit emblazoning of the cinematic aesthetic that consigns the erotic appeal of male beauty to the nostalgic, bereft form of the photograph.

On another wavelength, of course, the film's would-be Gramscian message has just been sounding as loudly as the factory whistle that punctuates it on the soundtrack. Ciro, embraced by his Milanese fiancée in the company of fellow workers, has achieved a manifestly PC—and all but PCI—social integration; he sketches out a still brighter prospect for Luca (Rocco

Vidolazzi), the youngest Parondi, in which the boy will return to a changed Lucania that has also been married to the modern forces of progress. But Luca is not seeing any of that; like us, he is hypnotized by the multitude of identical Roccos on display at the newsvendor's. And as he slowly—desultorily—passes these images, he does something at once simple-minded and psychotic: he starts to caress them, one after another, on the lips, the cheek, the forehead. Still beautiful Rocco! Might he not awaken even now, if, like a magic lamp, his photograph were rubbed the right way? Might all of them not awaken and form a mighty host? Luca thus disqualifies himself from being neorealism's prescribed signifier of the future, the future in which his longing for Rocco would be successfully dragooned, like the child army at the end of *Open City* (1945), into the

The people's homosexuality.

cause of universal human fellowship. Instead, he seems to be beginning—or rather for an instant resisting beginning—a painful apprenticeship to the closet-as-photograph. The grown-up workers he passes, also admiring the procession of Roccos, are naturally further advanced in training; like mature film spectators, they are more or less resigned to the fact that they are "just looking." Their lethargic witnessing is the quelled form of a political struggle based on libido rather than labor. Quite unlike Ciro with his old-Left boosterism, *Rocco* is finally only committed to brooding over the beautiful but blocked state of desire—and of cinema—that one might call the people's homosexuality.

6. *VERTIGO* (1958)

No way in.

THE FIRST TIME—in 1958, during the original release—was not happy. Though the vertigo shot made my head spin deliciously, it furnished my only thrill; the otherwise impenetrable yarn, by turns too slow-moving for my interest or too fast-paced for my understanding, had to be repeatedly explained to me by my mother afterward. I was disappointed at not finding the Hitchcock thriller I already knew, and incapable of appreciating the modernist art film that without warning had stolen its identity. (In this, apparently, I resembled the grown-ups around me; *Film Quarterly*, which, like *Vertigo*, first appeared in 1958, did not review it.) Since then, I have sat many times in movie theaters while *Vertigo* was being projected, have also purchased several versions of the film for my TV, PC, and iPhone. Yet despite such various second chances (of which another has just been offered me with Universal's new Legacy Series edition), I have little better idea of what *Vertigo* is about now than I did when I was ten years old; my ignorance has merely got stranger, because less explicable in an adult; it must seem, though it does not feel, like a phony trance. Was this first viewing—bored, restive, and uncomprehending—nonetheless so magnetic that it is drawing me still? Does it return, by some mundane memory trigger or mysterious unconscious agency, to repossess me?

There seems to be, in any event, no losing it. For though I now enter the temple called *Vertigo* with every intention of devotion, I soon start behaving like an ignorant and ill-behaved child made to sit through high mass. Irresistibly, my mind wanders, falls into daydreams or spins off into reminiscences related to the film by only the most finely customized tangents. And when, suddenly and for no good reason, something in the film—a line, a shot, a musical phrase—brings me back from these absent states, I hardly know what I regret more—losing the fiercely vivid pleasure that they afforded, or missing the master key to unlocking *Vertigo*, which I am convinced must have been proffered on screen just after I went off.

Naturally, I make frequent resolutions to watch *Vertigo* more responsibly, in a manner better suited to its status as perhaps the greatest film of them all. But even when I most doggedly concentrate on the images before me, I find myself sidetracked—staring at peripheral details, fixated on private, incommunicable nuances, or held in the grip of a camera movement much too long after it has passed. I am transfixed, for instance, by the pale iridescent steering wheel on Scottie's De Soto Firedome, which looks made from mother-of-pearl rather than plastic, and whose regular stippling seems to prescribe a firm and exact grip, as though, without such clenching, this exquisite thing of beauty would whirl away, out of control.

Scottie's steering wheel: plastic or mother-of-pearl?

Or I get as excited as a child with a new plaything by Midge's bright yellow Cosco stepstool, with retractable steps, just like the one we had in the kitchen at home, where it once furnished me both a staircase to climb up and a precipice to jump off. Or I marvel at how a clockwise pan of San Francisco yields to a counterclockwise pan of Madeleine's apartment building, conveying the thrilling impression that these two "spinning" shots, though successive, are somehow colliding; and my amazement only increases to find the second pan settling on an image that literalizes just such an imagined smash-up, with Madeleine's Jaguar screen-left (but pointing right) and a one-way street sign screen-right (but pointing left). In short, when I do succeed in focusing on *Vertigo*, all I see is just such a random series of little touches (never the same ones), and this fascination with "the small scenes, the fragments of the mirror" (as Scottie calls the disassembled details of Madeleine's dream), blinds me to even their immediate context, let alone what might hold them together.

Thus do I gaze at the summit of cinema: one eye, aversively farsighted, looks past the screen image to remoter regions of the mind, while the other, intently myopic, sees in this image nothing but small, unintegrated details. But on my most recent attempt at viewing *Vertigo*, a hypothesis occurred to me that, while of no help in correcting my addled eyesight, at least shifted the responsibility for it onto the film itself. Suppose, as I did, that my two impairments were to combine, that the eye that pulled away and the eye that drew forward *looked at the same time*. Wouldn't the resultant vision reproduce the famously disorienting shot used to present Scottie's vertigo, the shot in which the camera tracks back while zooming forward? Perhaps I don't see *Vertigo* because, in the effort to do so, I have contracted vertigo. Not the clinical inner-ear imbalance (from which, merciless in my medical ignorance, I used to tease my mother for suffering), but the formal ocular disturbance as defined—and practiced—by Hitchcock's film. And to judge by the symptoms of planar yo-yoing in William Friedkin's new commentary—where he identifies a through street as a cul-de-sac and confuses the tiles on the mission roof with the stones below it—I may not be alone.

■ ■ ■

After all, such distraction would be simply impossible with any other Hitchcock film. In *them*, we always know exactly where to direct our attention. Recall the signature dolly shot in *Notorious*, which sweeps down over the grand reception in progress to rest on a key in Alicia's hand. The camera's smooth, single-minded trajectory enjoins us to skim likewise over the staircase, the chandelier, the faces, the furniture—over everything but this key, which alone merits our scrutiny. Indeed, if some imp of the perverse led us to fix on any of these other things, our contrariness would be rewarded with nothing better than a generic swank-party background. For the most prominent object in a Hitchcock image is typically the most significant one as well. Alicia's key is also "key" in the figurative sense, its visual centrality clearly aligned with its narrative importance. It gets Devlin into the mysterious wine cellar where he proceeds to discover bottles of a vintage plot-thickener called uranium.

But in *Vertigo*, what is it that we are being asked to look at? "Madeleine" is the general answer to that question, of course, but Madeleine is in fact highly elusive. Even at first sight, Scottie does not see her directly, and after that, he tends to follow her from behind, so that we are only looking at the back of her head—or rather at her hairdo's black hole. Far from ever satisfying our gaze, Madeleine only entices us into trying to see something else, something in or beyond her, through the alluringly dark telescope embedded in her blonde chignon. We may call that something "Carlotta Valdez," but Carlotta is also unstable and fleeting; her face in the portrait differs from that of the figure she becomes in Scottie's nightmare, and in both, her hair is arranged in the same fascinating spiral style.

If the object of our attention is obscure and confused, moreover, so is the narrative logic it normally depends on. For all the garrulity of the exposition, it is never quite clear what following Madeleine is supposed to accomplish. Elster claims that he

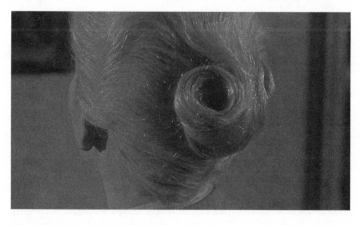

Madeleine's cyclopic coiffure . . .

. . . is also worn by Carlotta in the portrait.

The posy at Madeleine's side . . .

. . . is Carlotta's posy too.

needs to know where his wife goes before committing her to medical care, but as he seems already well-informed of Madeleine's unconscious identification with Carlotta, of what possible use to him is the banal list of San Francisco sights that is the only other thing Scottie's labors turn up? And by the time that Madeleine has jumped into San Francisco Bay, there is surely sufficient evidence to get her to a doctor. Just as the object's uncertainty implies its ultimate absence, so the plot's implausibility indicates the motivelessness at its core.

Accordingly, Hitchcock's suspense in *Vertigo* is deprived of its intelligibility. Either this suspense remains a vague haze, never condensing into its classically well-known forms, or else these same forms become formalities, emptied of any reason for their still rigorous observance. In the forest of giant redwoods, for instance, Madeleine suddenly runs away from Scottie and disappears, it seems, behind one of the tall trees. The scene then develops as a prolonged alternation between shots of Scottie looking for her and shots of the empty forest; astral music comes in to reinforce the ominous, otherworldly mood. But at the end of it all, there is Madeleine discovered standing against a tree just as we had commonsensically first supposed. The suspense, though obvious, is also gratuitous, giving us the impression that we have missed seeing something, or that what we have seen exceeds any possible point to it. No wonder my mind wanders as desultorily as Madeleine seems to do: I can't be sure what proper attention to *Vertigo* comprises, nor how such attention is rewarded. Still, as with Madeleine, some questions remain: Where do I go on my wandering? What takes me away?

■ ■ ■

Watching *Vertigo*, I am seized with a longing to visit San Francisco—an absurd feeling on two counts. For one thing, *Vertigo* renders the touristic idea of San Francisco with a repleteness that should leave nothing to be desired; the Golden Gate Bridge, the Palace of Fine Arts, the Legion of Honor Museum, Coit Tower, Mission Dolores—all shimmer in glorious Constable weather that a tourist seldom sees; and what a tourist always does see—the ignoble mass of his fellow gawkers—has been removed from every view. For another thing, I live in San Francisco; indeed, here I was born, raised, and taken to see *Vertigo* for the first time. What, then, could I possibly hope to see in San Francisco that has not already been given to my view either spectacularly, by the film itself, or mundanely, during my many years of inhabiting the place? But of course, it is from the clash, the mutual interference, of these two reasons that the irrational longing arises. Each San Francisco, by eclipsing my view of the other, makes me yearn to see "again," fully and distinctly, the prospect that it blocks.

Hitchcock's San Francisco (to start there) is a majestic abstraction of resplendent bridges, towers, palaces, and gardens, all grandly isolated, and all sumptuously empty. It is a kind of eerie mirage that, as a character in Wilde once said of San Francisco, "possesses all the attractions of the next world." Remarkably, however, the three main characters, dreamlike themselves, and gliding from wonder to wonder in cars fluent as gondolas, see no more of this unearthly city than their obsessive pursuits strictly require: precious little. No matter how spectacular the scenery at Fort Point or the Legion of Honor, Scottie has eyes for Madeleine only, while she, in making the full round of tourist sights, seems less to be seeing them than to be seeing *through* them to an ulterior world of which they are, at best, obscure intimations. Even Midge, would-be realist, ignores the classic view from her apartment window. The opposite of tourists, *Vertigo*'s characters couldn't care less about seeing the city that Hitchcock has made for them, but most fully depicts without them or behind their backs, in objective panoramas or rear projections.

That privileged class of tourist who is the film spectator should be perfectly positioned to enjoy what the characters miss. Yet despite the unsurpassed clarity of Robert Burks's photography, my vision of it is as negligent, as diverted by obsession, as that of Scottie, secretly watching Madeleine in the car ahead of his, or of Madeleine, still more secretly watching Scottie from her rear-view mirror—or with that eye in the back of her

Midge ignoring her classic view.

head—so as to prevent him from losing track of her. Always superimposed on *Vertigo*'s San Francisco are extraneous reflections of my own, unbidden memories that, in contrast to sightseers, can no more be banished from Hitchcock's images than Judy's vulgar accent and clothing can be purged from the ideal of Madeleine.

Some such memories are indefinite or even conjectural, shadowy souvenirs of the downtown wandering that I was allowed to do as a boy. But others are quite precise. In the sanatorium where Scottie is treated for "acute melancholia with a guilt complex," I recognize St. Joseph's Hospital where, in 1950s fashion, I had my tonsils removed, and where, after its much later condo-conversion, I lived for a while among buffed gay men who drove jeeps. At I. Magnin's, the high-end department store where Judy is employed, I too once worked, until the day when, whether dizzy from the scent, or just confused in the Christmas rush, I dropped a sample bottle of perfume, which shattered all over the floor. And at Ernie's, about the same time, I did my best to keep my cool while an entire meal, from the Steak Diane to the Cherries Jubilee, was flamed tableside for my prom date and me. Yet whether vague or detailed, the memories inevitably spoil Hitchcock's rigorously curated San Francisco by mock-heroically putting me into it. In the rarefied high-romantic ethos of *Vertigo*, this is not funny.

Recently, then, in an attempt to retrieve Hitchcock's San Francisco in all its unimpinged-upon purity, I treated myself to a thing called the Vertigo Tour, a private guided excursion through the locales of the film. At first it seemed to supply just what I was wanting. My guide would drive me, say, to

Mission Dolores, where we inspected the church and its garden, and then, as soon as we were back in the car, we would watch the correspondent scene from the film on a portable DVD player. At the pace we worked, the location never had the time to acquire much independent density; it capitulated easily to its instant virtualization. I was reminded of the series of shots at the Legion of Honor in which Scottie looks at Madeleine while she is looking at the portrait of Carlotta; he sees the posy at Madeleine's side, then sees it held by Carlotta in the portrait; he sees Madeleine's cyclopic coiffure, then sees it on Carlotta, too. These shots seal Scottie into the belief that Madeleine is, or thinks she is, possessed by Carlotta's spirit; and as my guide, following a similar procedure, reduced local sights to their Hitchcockian essence, I felt sutured into *Vertigo*'s San Francisco as never before. In one case, the location itself seemed to help the process along: the Empire Hotel, where Judy resides in the film, having long since become the York Hotel, was now being transformed once more, this time into the Hotel Vertigo.

But then, my guide offered to take me to a locale never seen in the film, but merely mentioned: the Portals of the Past in Golden Gate Park, a small portico by a lake where, as Elster tells Scottie, Madeleine likes to sit staring into space. I immediately recognized, though I hadn't revisited it since childhood, the lake where my father used to take me to feed "the duckies," who were still there, as Scottie would have said. And there *I* was—confused, distressed, and burdened with the added task of having to conceal these emotions from my guide—back in the raw mental state of being-distracted-from-*Vertigo*. With this difference: I now understood that my state of distraction was a way, albeit a tendentious one, of watching *Vertigo* nonetheless; and that all the while I thought my attention was wandering, it was scrutinizing, it was sifting the film for something that felt just on the verge of appearing on screen. I do not know what to call this thing exactly (me? my Carlotta?), but it must bear on the fact that, during the many years when *Vertigo* had been withdrawn from circulation and was being slowly prepared for its apotheosis, at the end of them, as a peerless cinematic masterpiece—during this Great Confinement, the film was also becoming a sort of filmic madeleine of San Francisco during my childhood. No wonder I can never find Hitchcock's San Francisco in any fullness; I am too busy, in my reveries, looking for my own, as if *Vertigo* were, of all things, a documentary. This is no doubt why I am held spellbound by the rear projections, which, for all their artifice, attest to the most indulgent location-shooting Hitchcock ever allowed himself. It is also why these are never quite satisfying: they never show me that archaic object, whatever it is, which always appears to be just out of sight.

If my desire to find *Vertigo* in San Francisco led me on the Vertigo Tour, my desire to find San Francisco in *Vertigo* took me on another, more simply managed journey: to my parents' house in the Outer Mission—a neighborhood on the wrong side of the tracking shots—in order to see my mother's yellow kitchen stepstool that, still retained, had now been relegated to the basement, near my old bedroom. Belonging to both Hitchcock's fiction and my reality, the chair would be the means of validating the one by the other, the link by which to identify

The yellow kitchen stepstool.

the one *as* the other. (And the chair is not all that peripheral a detail, I reminded myself; when Scottie stands on it, he experiences his first post-traumatic attack of vertigo, and Midge buries her catalogue copy of the "Portrait of Carlotta" beneath a pillow on its seat, almost as if she were interring it there.)

Yet this second adventure ended up being as futile as the first: for though I photographed the chair in various promising poses, even moving it back up to the kitchen, nothing made it *look* like the same chair. The resemblance was exact except for one element whose absence cancelled out all the others: fictionality. Only with this—as in an episode of *Mad Men*, where the yellow chair reappears in Peggy's lower-middle-class apartment—would the likeness be persuasive. Without it, the chair looked ridiculous, as I did on top of it—or as Midge does when she paints herself, complete with glasses and wry looks, into the portrait of Carlotta.

Midgelotta.

■ ■ ■

Eventually I started to suspect that neither my wandering attention to *Vertigo* nor my search for the film off-screen was merely a
personal failing; that, in the end, *Vertigo* not only permitted, but
also compelled bad spectatorship. Or, at any rate, in *one* of the
ends. For *Vertigo* has two endings: the one we know and the one
Hitchcock cut from the film during post-production. The latter,
called the "foreign censorship ending," may be found among
the extras on the Legacy release, where it is introduced with
the following advisory: "Hitchcock was required to shoot this
extended ending to satisfy the needs of the foreign censorship
committee. Were it not for this, he would never have allowed
it to be created. Seeing this footage, we can understand that he
was absolutely correct." So, with this lame explanation, the censorship ending is itself censored, judged external to Hitchcock's
authorship, and wrong for the film in any case; we may see it

only on condition that we do *not* see it as a valid or authentic part of *Vertigo*. Similar thinking caused it to be passed over in the Robert Harris/James Katz 1996 restoration work, so that it even *looks* negligible. Yet, though little regarded in both senses of the word, it remains a precious material exhibit of what I should call "unseen *Vertigo*" or "the *Vertigo* just out of sight."

The extended ending takes up where the familiar ending leaves off. From Scottie on his tower, it shifts to Midge in her apartment, where, on the night of the same day, she is anxiously listening to the radio: "Elster was last heard of living in Switzerland, but is now thought to be residing somewhere in the south of France. Captain Hansen states that he anticipates no trouble in having Elster extradited . . . once he is found." This, we suppose, is the moral denouement that a censorship committee might have required; but so feeble a promise of the criminal's punishment is persuasive only in its suggestion that, like Madeleine, his creation, and Scottie, his dupe, Elster too may have started to wander. The announcer himself then divagates to a very different item: "Other news on the local front: in Berkeley, three University of California sophomores found themselves in a rather embarrassing position tonight when they were discovered by Police Officer William Fogarty leading a cow up the steps of Legrand—." Here, Midge turns off the radio, but we have heard enough. We know the mischief intended by this once-common college prank: cows are incapable of walking on steps, which cause them panic and confusion. These wanton boys were seeking to induce a case of what can only be called *bovine vertigo*, the stupid, depsychologized version of Scottie's own predicament. And only now, against this literally unseen "comic relief," does Scottie enter the room; he takes up the drink Midge has mixed for him, and, turning his back on her and us alike, goes over to the window where—for the first time—he looks out, straight ahead, at the view of San Francisco: the end.

In the classical aesthetics referenced by the film's numerous neoclassical architectural forms, the comic relief provided by the woozy cow must seem so out of place as to be deservedly put out of sight as well. To my ill-aspected viewing, though, its value lies precisely in disturbing the *tragic relief* that the authorized ending clearly aims to provide. There, his hands forlornly held out, as if Judy had fallen through their fingers, Scottie looks like a piece of academic sculpture; indeed, his whole doleful attitude has been raised up like a monument and isolated in distinct outline from the rear-projected world around him. Such tragic standing implies a certain revelatory knowledge: Scottie can finally look down from on high and see clearly; he has been, in Friedkin's final words as commentator, "cured of his acrophobia." Corrected, Scottie's vision would now approximate the transcendental gaze often assumed by the camera in classic cinema—indeed, his POV, were it given here, would be an overhead shot like those Hitchcock himself frequently used to play up his mastery. In his despair, Scottie at least enjoys one comfort: a tragic hero, he is no longer a dizzy one.

By contrast, the extended ending removes him from the ennobling tower platform and brings him home to Midge's flat—and implicitly, to a drunk-and-depressed life with this altogether "wrong" version of Madeleine. But the important difference here is the return of San Francisco, which, for a change, we're not allowed to see very well. The nocturnal opacity is apt, for in this spectacle of a city as latent with vertigo as the wood decors of *Marnie* are with red, Scottie is also gazing at the matrix of Madeleine's vacant-eyed madness, which we may now recognize as his vertigo's extreme form. As Elster in fact tells Scottie, Madeleine's derangement began on the day when she saw San Francisco for the first time. "She was like a child come home. And when she came upon something unchanged, something that was as it had been, her delight was so strong, so fiercely possessive! These things were *hers* . . . Then one day a great sigh settled on her, and the cloud came into her eyes." Or rather, these are his words from the screenplay in which, unseen, he was scripted to voice them while Scottie was trying, and failing, to see Madeleine full-on at Ernie's. Hitchcock eliminated the speech along with the ending that so evocatively correlates to it. Otherwise, under the aegis of "San Francisco," *Vertigo*

No way out.

would have ended by insisting on a certain *cloudy* quality that abides in Scottie's looking, its unexhausted and even reawakened capacity for drifting into states of fascination, distraction, bewilderment, blindness—in short, for seeing badly.

"It's not funny," Scottie says of the portrait of Midgelotta, but of course, as no audience ever fails to prove, it *is*; Midge herself is a bit giddy with giggling as she finishes it up. And her first response to Scottie's assignment from Elster—to the plot's most basic assumption—has been to laugh out loud: "Oh, come on!" Similarly, the extended ending brings out the vertiginous farce, half Feydeau, half Punch-and-Judy, that underlies—and undermines—*Vertigo*'s towering tragedy. In doing so, this ending mounts a deadly *un*serious resistance to the desire for significance that marks not only *Vertigo*, but also, more wholeheartedly, its forbiddingly solemn critical celebration. Far from undertaking a cure, it reinstates the impairments of sight and sense that have been inextricable from Hitchcock's strange narrative, and whose idiosyncratic equivalents in any given viewing may hold the key to our common embarrassment in following *Vertigo*'s drift.

NOTE

The author gratefully acknowledges Mr. Jesse Warr, his guide on the Vertigo Tour.

7. *LA RONDE* (1950)

Le meneur de jeu: "I'm not part of the game. I run the ronde."

THE WHORE fucks the Soldier, the Soldier fucks the Maid, the Maid fucks the Young Master, and so on until, to end the rigmarole, the Count fucks the Whore, and what seemed to be an interminable line warps into an all-encompassing circle: that is the memorable structure of Arthur Schnitzler's *Reigen* ("Round Dance"). Everywhere you turn, the same unsavory little story: the triumph of the sex drive, whose blunt insistence destroys its idealization as love. Copulation organizes each episode; a *double* copulation organizes the series. Though men want one thing only, they never want it from the same woman, and vice versa; the dance obliges everyone to change partners. In this unsparingly disenchanted vision, copulation even lacks discernible purpose. The characters don't seem to *have* sex so much as sex *has them*, using them parasitically as host-environments for its reproduction. Not that such reproduction is tied to procreation, or the "passing of the sperm," as David Thomson believes; *Reigen* repeatedly confronts the facts of life, but hardly once mentions the making of babies that the facts of life are normally brought forward to explain. Stripped of its halos, alibis, and consequences, sex would constitute a cruel, if pleasurable, formalism whose sole principle is sex for sex's sake. And with the closing of the circle, the final, surprising, yet not unexpected, match of high and low, such urgent but empty and gratuitous sex seems a universal fate.

In all likelihood, the outrage caused by *Reigen*'s first performance owed less to the on-stage acknowledgment of sex than to the *idea* of sex that it demonstrated—namely, the idea of sex as an insult, an insult to all the social, psychological, and biological moralisms with which we normally domesticate it.

Revolving door.

But the turns of sexual history have visited a strange fate on *Reigen*. As the play's shocking para-Freudian propositions about sex have succeeded in becoming *idées reçues*, its arena of permissiveness must now strike us as much less unruly, and far more circumscribed, than it once did. Tellingly, the play recognizes impotence, but not perversion; sex here has no other form but the textbook Fuck, the primal act whose commission confers on a Man and a Woman their profound and indeed only truth. Anything else is not even foreplay; it is just bad faith. So tightly wound is *Reigen* around the heterosexual couple's doing what comes naturally that the narrative, far from scandalous now, looks like a manual of normativity, a canned celebration of "classic sex." In the course of one too many sexual revolutions, *Reigen* has reeled over to the *ancien régime*.

■ ■ ■

It is the first merit, then, of Ophuls's *La Ronde* (1950) to have understood this basic problem facing cinematic adaptation of *Reigen*. Even in 1950, when the film was being shot, Schnitzler's material had ceased to be obscene; indeed, it was already in the dismal condition of *what used to be sexy*. Ophuls develops *La Ronde*'s great poetry not around desire, therefore, but around the anhedonia of a world in which desire survives only as an antique sign of itself, a memorial tombstone laid over its grave. He supplements the even pairs of Schnitzler's round dance with a singleton: a man of the world, mature and wise, so discreet and doleful and correctly dressed that, though he is ostensibly brought in to serve as a master of ceremonies, to "animate" the ronde, he might equally pass for an undertaker, come to lay it out properly. In whichever role, this *meneur de jeu* (Anton Walbrook), as critical tradition calls him, announces episodes, assigns partners, facilitates rendezvous, and forestalls catastrophes; as an emblem of this labor, he is often shown running— and on one occasion repairing—a small, decoratively sluggish merry-go-round.

The addition of an uncompanioned auxiliary transforms the Schnitzlerian ethos completely. *Reigen*'s dance had seemed to proceed with perfect spontaneity, the natural expression of a sex drive that flowed as abundantly as a river in spate; *La Ronde*'s merry-go-round has become a bit of a grind, requiring the MJ's continual maintenance to keep its wheels greased and turning. It has also now become the object of his gaze, which, however fascinated by—and even necessary to—its operations, can never wholly disappear into them; he is typically shown observing the battle of the sexes with eyes askant and head slightly cocked. The emphasis on his off-angled vantage comes as early as the opening shot sequence, in which, after introducing himself, he suggestively passes a theater stage and a movie set to enter what he identifies as "Vienna, 1900," and where, changing into a tailcoat, he proceeds to the merry-go-round and sets it going. This famously long take is linear, a not unimportant first fact in a film called *La Ronde* (always misremembered for the circular camera movements of which it in fact contains practically none); still more significantly, this line touches the carrousel only tangentially, insisting on the MJ's spatial as well as temporal remove. The shot so often adduced as our serpentine induction into a waltz-like erotic whirl puts us strictly on the sidelines.

Viewed from there, the ronde becomes sad as an elegy and boring as a rerun. In turn-of-the-century Vienna, where *Reigen* was written as well as set, its scandalous sexual vignettes had an aggressive contemporary character, and their "degeneracy" qualified them even better as the last word in modernity. In *La Ronde*, this Vienna offers no more than a quaint sexual mythology, a rococo love hotel that features champagne suppers in *cabinets particuliers* and canopied beds with Stendhal's *De l'amour* gracing the nightstands. "I adore the past," says the MJ, "it's so much more restful than the present and so much more certain than the future." Certain and restful: desiderata for a good night's sleep, no doubt, but hardly a practicable recipe for the other thing people do in bed. And if the opening long take does not perform the circular motion attributed to it, the film's indisputable on-screen rotations—the carrousel, a Ferris wheel, a revolving door, a waltzing couple, and even a pair of bicycles—protest too much with their naughty insinuation of "screwing"; they more successfully convey the reassuring calm of nicely regulated clockwork. In less time than it takes for Oscar Straus's theme waltz to become an ineradicable earworm—that is to say: on the very instant of their first presentation—the episodes and characters have "turned" in a quite different sense: they have curdled into stereotypes. Not even the "illicit" character of most of the episodes can kick them up; this is nothing but the *sanctioned illicit* of the nineteenth-century bourgeois order, already fully codified in its literature, where the only thing more "correct" than a young master initiating himself with the chambermaid is that, in later life, when he has become a *père de famille*, he keep a young mistress on the side.

Small wonder that we chuckle complacently when the camera cuts from a nascent sex scene between the Actress (Isa Miranda) and the Count (Gérard Philipe) to a shot of the MJ, with celluloid and scissors, supposedly editing out of the film the couple's further progress. Not at all aroused by the sex scene in the first place, we don't feel in the least cheated when it is truncated. The act of censorship only tells us, of palpable eroticism, how little there would ever be to censor in *La Ronde*. But though this sequence does not sexually excite or frustrate us, it does do something for which our biddable laughter offers thanks: it flatters our sexual sophistication.

Such would appear to be the second labor of the MJ: to be *knowing* and to spread his knowingness around: not so much to the characters whom he advises and consoles, but who remain rather dense about it all, as to the spectators whom he invites to

What is being censored?

imitate him and the critics who—see Terence Rafferty's super-
suave essay in the Criterion booklet—are generally happy to
parade their own similarly melancholy *savoir vivre*. The MJ
introduces himself thus: "I am the incarnation of your desire . . .
your desire to know everything." His self-correction, moving us
from our desire to a desire to know everything about it, identifies a sour project that we hear very little about in criticism of
La Ronde: to replace erotic experience with that "experienced"
attitude toward it that is in fact its depressive antithesis. Yet with
erotic experience overfamiliarized from the start, how could we
ever *not* be knowing about it? The MJ's knowingness is too easy
not to be facile, less the fruit of experience than its evasion;
it refuses to recognize the underlying sexual numbness—his,
theirs, ours—that it rationalizes and extends. As a result, his

sophisticated *répliques* seem hardly distinguishable from the hackneyed desire he purports to know all too well.

■ ■ ■

Yet despite his claim that *La Ronde* is "everyone's story," it's manifestly not *his*. To the Prostitute (Simone Signoret) coming on to him, he says, "There must be some mistake, Madame. I'm not part of the game. I run the ronde." From this ostensibly universal structure, its own managing director has been excluded. The contradiction is never seen as one; but how does something so obvious, so flatly stated, get to pass for invisible? Partly because Author (or Director) and Character are felt to occupy distinct worlds, with different laws applying—and partly owing to the reinforcing distinction between Desire, felt by the blinkered characters who ride the ronde, and Knowledge, distilled in the celibate MJ who runs it. But the wit of Ophuls's conceit depends on the constant *breaching* of levels between the story and its framing; the MJ is pictured now as part of the story being filmed (a coachman, a waiter, a neighbor), now as part of its filming, with scissors or clapboard in hand. And however flat the ronde's erotics, they elicit from him a performance so overflowing with animation, anxiety, invention, and ruse, that no word *but* desire can describe the oddity of its excess. Indeed, this is the only desire in the film that is cut fresh off the bone. It is accounted for neither in terms of the desire circulating *on* the carrousel, which the MJ doesn't share, nor by the knowledge circulating *about* the carrousel, which comprehends everyone's desire but his own. In the glib machinery of *La Ronde*, the MJ is the loose screw.

But you would never know this from the scholarly commentaries produced for the Criterion edition, which allow the MJ no space as a desiring being, with a sexual center or even an erotic surface. Susan White observes that a man and a woman who have made love are "reduced to the essentials of their species," while in a similar spirit, Alan Williams, the other authorized talker, remarks that the symmetries of Ophuls's style are "structured on gender roles" (as if these were symmetrical!). And by commissioning this pairing of Williams and White, by conjoining them like one more "symmetrical" and essentialized couple on the carrousel, Criterion would assure us that the treatment of sexuality in the film is balanced and, so to speak, well-rounded.

Amid such unseeing hetero-narcissism, one must be grateful for the openly homophobic joke that Daniel Gélin tells about Walbrook in a 1989 interview reissued among the supplements:

The Friday or Saturday before filming was to begin on Monday, Max went to see Anton. They'd known each other for ages. He said, "I don't know how to say this. It's quite awkward. Anyway, you know what I mean. You don't really like women. You're more attracted to . . ." Anton said, "I understand. You're afraid I'll look too queer. Just say it!" Ophuls says, "Yes, that's it!" Anton says, "It's very simple. During rehearsals and shooting, if I forget to act 'manly,' you and I will simply agree on a code. The moment you think it's too apparent, that my [Gélin stumbles on the next word, as if it were a tongue-twister—or a potential confession] homosexuality is too obvious, just cough and I'll understand."

The weekend passed and Anton shot his scenes, but he sort of forgot. And there were moments where it was clear as day [Gélin laughs]. Max began quietly coughing. [Gélin coughs in imitation]. But Anton kept right on, he had forgotten their signal. Max's coughs got louder, but Anton went right on. [Gélin coughs louder] Finally, Anton, who'd completely forgotten, goes up to him and asks, "What's wrong, Max? Coming down with a cold?" [Laughter to indicate the story is over; the interview too has concluded.]

This anecdote is illustrated with clips from Walbrook's performance: moments that we are invited to read as exemplifying those blatant homosexual lapses, those obvious but self-oblivious revelations that reduced poor Max to coughing and now ask us to share Gélin's laughter. "Who am I? People never know more than a piece of reality; why? Because they see only one side of things"; these words, though scripted by Ophuls, now seem to lay bare the actor's sexual orientation, as if literally exposing his behind. And when, to show that he sees things "from all sides, in the round," Walbrook waves a circle in the air with his overlimber wrist, throwing an appraising glance at his fingernails, we seem to have caught him in the act of making the classic homosexual slip.

A nasty, irresponsible, and untrustworthy air hangs over this interview segment. But over the better-behaved commentary, with its sins of omission only, it has the advantage of showing that the MJ's exclusion from the sexuality of the ronde is not the same thing as his exclusion from sexuality. For who is not immediately convinced by Walbrook's swish hand—or by a whole archipelago of such moments that, on this hint, we may readily discover extending all through his performance— of the existence of a different MJ from the one we have been narrowly allowed to know? This new MJ is not the regretful Spirit of Sex Past haunting the antique carrousel; nor is he the arch sophisticate who, like you, knows everything about sex and feels nothing; he is instead an incorrigible queen, whose super-refinement—however cleverly it embellishes the heterosexual circuit—betrays the bad form of his sexual eccentricity.

That Walbrook should appear to "forget to act manly" is, whatever else, the inevitable effect of his structural position in *La Ronde*; and had Gélin assumed the role, he too would have leaked suspicious signs of one sort or another. In *Reigen*, of course, there could *be* no perversion; nothing else existed but the Fucking

Mechanical rotation.

Heterosexual Couple. But in *La Ronde*, this dyad requires for its unity an excluded third, who, unmatched with any partner, must seem (once we see him as at all sexual) to represent perversion in its purest form. Yet let's not mince our mincer: while others might play heterosexuality's excluded third (the spinster, the celibate, the "dirty" old man, the pedophile, even the child), for whom but the homosexual is this the role of a lifetime?

Look again at the celebrated shot in which the carrousel spins in one direction while a couple waltzing in the foreground (Danielle Darrieux as the Young Wife and Gélin as the Young Master) turns in the other; the camera slowly moves sideways, once again in tangent to the ronde, and then approaches Walbrook, shown from a low angle looking on. Superficially, the contrast is between the couple's fluent movement and his upright rigidity; but if you look more closely, you will see that the waltzers are not really moving at all; they are being rotated mechanically on a platform, and even their conversation is obviously faked "business." By contrast, Walbrook's apparent inertness proves to be the restraint of a magnificent economy of action. He has been holding up a cane, which he lets drop with perfect timing just as he also drops the dampening news that the lovely Young Wife is about to sleep with . . . her Husband (Fernand Gravey). And in the grain of his cryptic expression, variously eager, tired, absorbed, indifferent, aloof, resigned, you may read a whole unwritten volume of twentieth-century sexual history. This is the bright-eyed/indrawn face of one who must enliven the ronde with his wit and taste, but remain on its perimeter, excluded from participation; the fascinated/bored look of one who must always be *just* looking, whose erotic options are

Perfect timing.

restricted by the ronde to self-monitoring narcissism or servile voyeurism; the commanding/cowed attitude of one who takes vengeance on the ronde with his *irony*, half spiteful, half serene, and refuge from it in his impeccable, or embarrassing, but in any case unassimilable *style*. It will always seem reductive to see the MJ, through Walbrook's performance, as "gay." But how much more reductive *not* to see this, to see only the ronde instead of *La Ronde*.

8. *THE H-MAN* (1958)

I REMEMBER seeing *The H-Man* on television one late evening in early adolescence; it was a silly specimen of an already cheesy 1950s genre, the "made in Japan" sci-fi/horror film. As usual, the hydrogen bomb served as *fons malorum*, but this time, it didn't produce giant monsters that terrified entire populations; it merely turned a few sailors into modestly scaled streaks of watery slime that went about melting people, one by one. It was as if the threat of atomic holocaust were being carried out by a small gang of serial killers. No self-respecting teenager, especially if he were also a young gentleman cinephile who considered the movie below his station, could resist pouring scorn on its feeble conceit—along with its trite characterizations, stilted dialogue, absurd science, and just *pitiful* special effects.

But a DVD explosion has caused *The H-Man* to mutate into a beautiful and genuinely harrowing new form: its original one as *Bijo to ekitainingen* (*Beauty and Liquid Human*, 1958).[1] The film now runs to its full length in proper TohoScope proportion, has thrown off its black-and-white rags for regal technicolor (who knew?) and speaks fluent Japanese instead of cartoon English. In the metamorphosis, *Liquid Human* may have also become recognizable as one of classic cinema's great fantastic tales. But if I can't say so with certainty, that's because a curious mental deliquescence overcame me as I watched it; the film's conceit, to which I had once given a stony welcome, now affected me to excess. I found myself absorbed in the film, and yet unable to concentrate on it. It compelled me, but only to stand by and watch as it dissolved the normal organization of my attention. References commingled, categories blurred, and standards collapsed in confusion; among other casualties, the distinction between a frog and a prince had ceased to be watertight.

To begin with, I hardly knew what kind of film I was watching as *Liquid Human* slithered from one genre to another. This nominal sci-fi/horror successively absorbed the gangsters, girls, and detectives of a film noir; the deserted ship and melancholy blue specters of a ghost story; even the chanteuse and dance troupe of a musical. Perhaps the generic fluidity was part of what triggered my vivid, quasi-hallucinatory sense that other films were being streamed into my viewing, including some that lacked any serious or even sensible relation to *Liquid Human*. Amid the flux, I found myself seeing Ozu's *Early Autumn* for no better reason than that I recognized Yumi Shirakawa from that film as Chikako Arai, the chanteuse in this one. And in the eerie twang that composer Masaru Sato used to herald Liquid Human's approach, I heard his earlier score for *I Am Waiting*, a 1957 "Nikkatsu noir." With still more slickness, the ghosts in

Streaming associations.

Liquid Human conjured up *Ugetsu* and *Throne of Blood*, while the sewers extended all the way back to *The Third Man* and Raymond Bernard's *Les Misérables*. At the beginning, when heavy showers drenched the Tokyo streets, the title number of *Singin' in the Rain* was also being performed; and next to the too-traumatized-to-be-heteronormative couple at the end, there were Mitch and Melanie from *The Birds*. These dubious collations presented themselves to me as peremptorily as sidebars spring up on a webpage. *Liquid Human* had my attention "running," without rule or propriety, all over the place.

Such intertextual association, of course, lies latent in every viewing; an implicit sense of a film's resemblance-and-difference to others is a very condition of its intelligibility. Normally, though, a viewer keeps the process within bounds; having winnowed the deliberate from the fortuitous, and the meaningful from the irrelevant, he lets the chaff be still. What felt odd to me was not the capricious or contingent character of my associations, but my incapacity to keep them in their rightfully marginal place. And even less did I know what to do with the undeniable gratification I took in all this. After all, *Liquid Human* was granting me what my favorite art films were too special, too distinctively themselves, to have ever allowed: a deliriously glib vision of *virtual cinema*: an endless flux of images from all the films I had ever seen, or could imagine. Yet though I liked my new fluidity, I didn't like liking it. It had taken away my critical discrimination, and I regretted no longer being, as they used to say, a man of parts.

■ ■ ■

In the cruelty of youth, I deemed *The H-Man* as vacant of substance as those overcoats, suits, and uniforms that the H-Man, having dissolved a man's flesh, left lying behind. But youth can be cruel in many ways, and I also found the film, despite my best sarcastic intentions, intolerably sexy. What particularly inflamed my mind, and threatened to dissolve my too-solid flesh into a goo (incredible as this must sound to those unversed in the fanatically discreet ways that 1950s cinema ministered to sexual fantasy) was precisely those same overcoats, suits, and uniforms. For they are vacant because—or so the police at first suppose—the gangsters fleeing in them have "run away naked." Left lying first on the street—then on the stairs—then on the futon—they are thus place-holders for the male body imagined to have just slipped out of them: not only the dissolved body, invisible because it cannot be *seen*, but also the denuded body, invisible because it cannot be *shown*. The film soon takes this provocative doubleness into its very plot: the cleverest gangster, Uchida (the *beau-laid* Makoto Sato), throws his clothes into a heap and, while the police conclude he has been liquefied, waits tensely in the shadows, packing nothing but heat. As for the liquefaction process itself, Eiji Tsuburaya's special effects render it in yet more suggestive terms. He replaced the actors (for Liquid Human's victims are almost exclusively male) with balloons, giving the flesh an added turgidity and making its detumescence all the more spectacular as the air—along with the juice—pours out of them. This, in short, was what my adolescence had shamefully discerned in *The H-Man*: a homosexuality hidden in the respectability of suits and ties, and practiced under cover of a large mushroom cloud responsible for all sorts of abnormalities.

In *Beauty and Liquid Human*, the very title announces the dominant heterosexual orientation that I had overlooked but now find as obvious as I did the homosexual subtext. As one character tells us straight out, every man in the film—gangster, detective, or scientist, young or old, handsome or homely—is

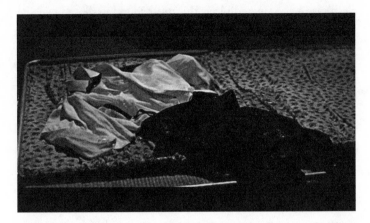

Liquefied.

Detumescing.

"after" the titular beauty, Chikako. And in the course of absorbing many of these admirers, Liquid Human comes to be after her too as its last, best prize. The coded homosexuality would be neutralized accordingly as a sort of male bonding, the gradual elimination and consolidation of rivals in preparation for a final attack on "the" woman. At the film's climax, Uchida drags Chikako down into the sewers, where he offers her an ostensibly stark choice: be his girl, or be dissolved by Liquid Human. But it's the same difference: mauling this beauty and melting her seem equivalent sexual aims. They also appear to be the *only* ones where she is concerned. Though Dr. Masada (Kenji Sahara) wins Chikako by protecting her from both outcomes, this boyish hero hardly counts as a mature male. Even as it is, he must be wounded on his chivalric quest, his blood let on the same principle by which leeches were formerly applied to cool down the febrile body, or calm down the overexcited one; unsurprisingly, his first act on rescuing Chikako is to put more clothes on her.

■ ■ ■

All this is the very stuff of mainstream representation, but something has polluted the stream. Much of what I missed the first time around was in fact *missing*: the American version had been censored. Columbia Pictures, the U.S. distributor, didn't simply change the film's title, so as to eliminate its luridly mythic opposition between female beauty and a bestial human liquid; it also edited out some of its most intense images, which only now, fifty years later, we can see.

The main object of this censorship was, curiously, the liquefaction of Liquid Human's only female victim: Emi (Ayumi Sonoda), the "cheap" Chikako-proxy who is the club's lead dancer. Two shots were eliminated. Like the male victims, Emi leaves her clothes behind, but what remains on the floor in her case is not a boxy suit or coat, but the sequined bra-and-panty costume she performs in. The deletion of this image perhaps requires little explanation; given the targeted audience of normal American boys, it was doubtless considered too precise an evocation of female nudity. The more puzzling case is the shot of Emi's actual liquefaction that was removed as well. For this, Tsuburaya created a unique special effect. The outline of Emi's body, instead of collapsing, remains intact, as a freeze frame insists we notice. At the same time, through the introduction of animation into this frame, the flesh is shown being gradually replaced, from the bottom up, with a bubbling green liquid. This may indeed be the sexiest moment in the film, but it is certainly the weirdest as well; what its sexiness consists in is by no means easily assimilable to conventional paradigms. And though 1950s Japanese horror films suffered a variety of indignities before they were released in the U.S. (such as, famously, the replacement of the Japanese reporter with a white American in the 1954 *Godzilla*), the removal of a gruesome special effect was not among them; such horrors sold the movie.

The shot, then, needs to be looked at more closely (chapter 18). Right before it, we have seen the greenish Liquid Human puddling at the feet of Emi's lover (himself just liquefied), then surging up her legs. Perhaps, with this implicit heterosexual allegory in mind, the Columbia censors saw the subsequent special effect as spelling it out; they saw, in other words, Emi's body being filled up, like a glass, with the Liquid Human that was pouring out of her lover. But that is not in fact what we see here. Emi's body is not filled up, but *covered over*. In this sense, it is all

Emi's new outfit.

Useless castoffs.

the odder that the shot was censored because the covering-over is already censorship of a classic kind; we see much less of Emi's body than before, and the uniform green ooze blots out the erogenous markers central to heterosexually organized excitement. The trouble with Emi's empty costume was merely the overexplicitnesss of thus "undressing" her; the more serious trouble with Emi's liquefaction is the indefinition that results from a certain way—neither modest nor "provocative"—of *dressing* her.

We should not dismiss this image as a technically primitive special effect that Tsuburaya, with today's CGI, would have corrected so that Liquid Human came unmistakably *in* Emi and not *on* her. The disturbing—and disturbingly sexy—quality of the image lies precisely in the fact that neither the attack nor its object is *heterosexual enough*. The green caress does not penetrate Emi's body, which in turn becomes nothing more than an effervescent surface. Her new skin—but can we call it "hers," or even "his"?—does not recognize genitalia, erogenous zones, or even different body parts. The costume's sequins seem to be sparkling everywhere on this skin, whose only variegation is provided by the shifting patterns and intensities of its ebullience. In this garish but gripping light, the bra and panties left behind seem the useless cast-offs of a libido that has ceased to recognize them as the metonyms of its sole theater of operations. Emi's liquefaction might be thought of as visualizing what Gilles Deleuze calls "the body without organs": a body released from the grip of sex organs and orientations, and transformed into a field of radical perversity whose multiple excitements can be entertained anywhere, anyhow.

Here, of course, Deleuze's utopia of sexual disintegration wears the aspect of horror—the feel is sexy but does anyone want to look like this? Yet in a horror film, the horror can never be just horrible; its repellence is the royal road to our absorption in it. Thus, though we are grateful to see the cutaway shot of Chikako in a strapless gown putting on lipstick—a quick reaffirmation of the classically partitioned heterosexual object—we are more grateful to see Liquid Human again, now of ambiguated gender, as it slides up the powder-room wall to threaten her with Emi's fate.

This continual wavering between classic sex and libidinal virtuality finds its objective correlative in Liquid Human itself. Though the creature typically appears as a sort of slime torpedo, it also takes two other forms that isolate its polarities. On the one hand, it appears as, simply, *human*. Those doleful blue specters, featureless of face, but definitely anthropomorphic in body, whom we see on board the abandoned ship are elegiac reminders of the mutant when it was still imaginable as having an ennobling human quality. On the other hand, it also appears as, simply, *liquid*. The slime torpedo not only finds its natural habitat

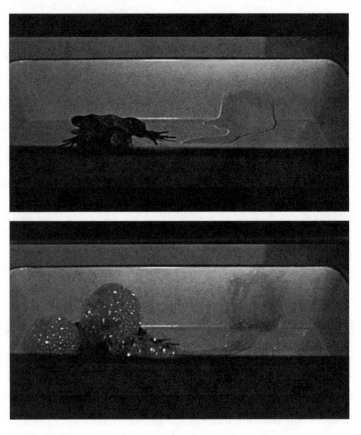

Froggy liquid.

in water, but also requires sea, sewer, river, and rainstorms to get about in the world. It thus turns every watery substance into a potential extension of its being. (Even "liquid refreshments" such as the vaguely sinister cocktails consumed at the club seem possible carriers; Uchida's clothes are found in a subterranean liquor storeroom, and the ship captain has disappeared in the midst of drinking a glass of whiskey that remains suggestively half-full on his table.) Such "mere" liquid no longer has any connection with the human at all; no ghost from the human past, it is the wave—upon wave upon wave—of an unhuman future.

The point is most forcefully made when, to demonstrate the origin of Liquid Human, Dr. Masada bombards a frog with radiation; the resultant froggy liquid is then put into a dish with a still-normal fellow amphibian, which melts on contact. But the liquid per se, familiarly green and bubbling, no more allows us to tell Liquid Frog from Liquid Human than the film lets us distinguish genre cinema from art-film intelligence. Ultimately, the film's monster of dissolution, not even species-specific, is perhaps better named just Liquid. As such, it stands in total opposition to the eponymous Blob in the American film also from 1958. The Blob, the poor man's Sartrian nightmare, mires its victims in the viscosity of things; Liquid, Deleuze's wet dream, does not murder, but melts; here human dignity is lost to going—or is it coming?—with the flow.

■ ■ ■

In the end, Liquid is a problem requiring resolution. "The only way we can fight it," says the Scientist in charge of the operation, "is with fire," water's symbolically antithetical substance. Appropriately, gasoline is released into the sewers and set ablaze. As the spreading conflagration gives Tokyo's waterways a blistering new skin, its efficacy at first seems straightforward; we see the slimy form of Liquid being seared, and the humanoid form being shrunken. Yet, as we eventually realize, we do *not* see the virtual form (as "the watery") misting away. (And if this did happen, we would only have got a sneak preview of *The Human Vapor*, the horror movie that Ishiro Honda, as if cycling mutancy through the four elements, made a year later.) The Scientist pronounces Liquid "as good as dead," but it looks more like Liquid has mutated into a river of fire that—as fire—will never be extinguished and that—as river—will never dry up.

With flames leaping over bridges and tall buildings, Liquid finally acquires the dimensions suitable to the Monstrous; and as these flames take possession of the entire visual field, it also finally offers a worthy image of the atomic holocaust that, in slime form, constrained to proceed by one body at a time, it had signally failed to represent. To clinch the point, Sato's juicy jazz track lapses into the shrill military march already heard during the H-bomb explosion that begins the film. We are being summoned back to attention. And attention must now again be paid as, over the final image of flames, the Scientist solemnly warns us of the possible extinction of humanity by the H-bomb.

Strangely, though, his warning feels too late, coming amid apocalyptic imagery that doesn't allow us to distinguish between atomic annihilation and anti-radioactive weaponry, or between

Puritan fire.

a spectacle of Liquid Triumphant and a scene of Liquid Being
Brought to Order. The conflation is the Liquid effect intended
to end all Liquid effects. For if it does not succeed in eliminat-
ing Liquid from Earth, it does manage to eliminate the libidinal from Liquid. In youth, I protected myself from the film's
over-palpable excitements with sarcasm; censors had already
done something similar through excision; but such expedients
are pale fire compared to the far more drastic option now taken
by the film itself. This is the "nuclear option" of fusing Liquid
to a single all-embracing devastation that would annul libido
in *every* form. To render Liquid even figuratively ("as good as")
dead, overkill is literally the order of the day; as the Scientist
insists, "*Any* suspicious areas must be burned." In this Hiro-
shima of Sex, libidinal mobility is tolerable only as the permanent mobilization against it.

NOTE

1. The new DVD gives us the choice of watching either the English-language version of *The H-Man* or the Japanese original. With a strange contempt, though, Sony has retained the export title for the DVD menu of both versions, and has not even subtitled the Japanese title when it appears on screen in the original version. Here I've chosen to use its literal translation, in the shortened form of *Liquid Human*. To Anglophone viewers, the "H" in *The H-Man* is no doubt quite expressive (of the Homo, the He-man, the Human, and the H-bomb, not to mention Horror and Hell); but *Liquid Human*, in suspending the antitheses between definite/indefinite, singular/plural, and male/female, names something more fundamental to the film.

9. FRENCH HITCHCOCK

THIS COLUMN originally began as a musing on the new Blu-ray edition of Hitchcock's *Psycho* (1960), which let me see previously invisible lines, pores, makeup on the actors' faces: the ageless film looked old at last. But I was thrown off my subject by the death of Claude Chabrol—or rather, by a certain (to me) striking detail in his necrology. The man known as the French Hitchcock had died at the age of eighty . . . just like Hitchcock. It was madness to be unnerved by this minor tabloidesque coincidence, but—we all go a little mad sometimes—it got under my skin. In my private ranking system, Chabrol had occupied the place of Favorite Working Filmmaker for a full thirty years. And now, as one after another obituary obliged me to read the words "the French Hitchcock" (often even in French!) I felt a frisson of horror—as if I were learning, along with the news of Chabrol's death, that he had died from a misnomer. My intervals of rationality did nothing to abate this horror; they merely replaced a superstitious belief that his epithet had murdered him with the positive knowledge that, as an epitaph now, it was robbing his grave.

It cheats him of his due distinction in two opposite ways. First, by suggesting that "Chabrol" is just French for "Hitchcock," it virtually guarantees incomprehension and disappointment: the spectator who comes to a Chabrol expecting a Hitchcock is sure to find it peculiarly off the mark, and will be that much less likely to identify this "off" quality as a deliberate, defining feature of its style. And second, by commonsensically implying that Hitchcock is not French, it dissembles an important historical fact: the Hitchcock whom we recognize and revere as cinema's supreme artist was born not in late-Victorian London but in mid-twentieth-century Paris, midwifed by the eager young critics at *Cahiers du cinéma*. It was in 1957, for instance, that two of them, Chabrol and Eric Rohmer, published the world's first book-length study of Hitchcock. Its claim that he was a major artist and the American period his major phase, its recognition of the fatal encounter and the psychic transference as central fantasies, its injunction that "it is in form that we must look for the depth of the work"—all this became and remains the basic operating equipment for thinking about Hitchcock. Long before anyone dreamed of calling him the French Hitchcock, Chabrol was one of those chiefly responsible for making Hitchcock French.

Yet what disturbed me more deeply than the falsity of Chabrol's journalistic tag was my old uncomfortable sense of its truth—a sense so sharply revived on his death that it caused me to feel that Hitchcock himself had died a second time.

For during the same thirty years (as it happens, the period that had elapsed since Hitchcock's death in 1980), I was as firmly persuaded that Chabrol was the Other Hitchcock as if I believed in metempsychosis. And if that were my mystic doctrine, it would have found validation in certain curious coincidences (as a Poe narrator might say) that took place in 1969. It was then that Hitchcock, not wishing to return to Paris to location-shoot a new ending for *Topaz*, entrusted the filming of the last shot to . . . Chabrol, whom he only slightly knew. The same year saw both the U.S. release of *Topaz* itself, a disaster that loudly heralded Hitchcock's artistic decline, and the French premiere of *La Femme infidèle* (The Unfaithful Wife), the first film in the great pentalogy of thrillers (the "Hélène cycle") that got Chabrol known as Hitchcock's French double.

Perhaps the hand-off was but a convenient working arrangement and perhaps such generational shifts in directors'

Hitchcock's stand-in.

reputations are common, even inevitable occurrences. And yet it all suggested to me something stranger—something like one of those weird interpsychic intimacies that Chabrol had identified in Hitchcock's films and was already wildly reproducing in his own. Was it truly just chance that Hitchcock's well seemed to be running dry just as Chabrol's showed early signs of over-flowing? Just chance that when Hitchcock no longer seemed artistically viable Chabrol began being called by his name? Just chance that *La Femme infidèle* consolidated Chabrol's style around its peculiar way of citing Hitchcock's? "Of course it was all just chance!" you will rightly retort. But that is only to say, with the hero of Chabrol's *This Man Must Die* (also 1969), that "chance is fantastic—and it exists."

No doubt, it is not simply random accident that defines the relationship between Hitchcock's films and Chabrol's—that enables the profuse textual transmigration that, once seen, is unmistakable. But nor can this process be satisfactorily explained as a deliberate project of imitation or homage. After all, he is not the Other Hitchcock who sets out to be. If there was any merit to Gus Van Sant's 1998 *Psycho* remake, with its perfidious fidelity to the original's shot structure, it consisted only in confirming the strength of Hitchcock's resistance to replication, a resistance so ferocious that it turned arguably the most frightening movie ever made into unquestionably the most boring remake. Of all those innumerable films since 1960 claiming to be "Hitchcockian," how many are like Hitchcock's? Or—a better question, to which the answer is nonetheless the same—how many are at all interestingly unlike them? Chabrol alone induced Hitchcock's stubbornly immovable spirit to pass into a different body of work. He did this, I think, by perfecting an extreme sensitivity to Hitchcock that—precisely as a mere sensitivity, a "thin skin" and nothing more—never acquired the consistency of an emotional attitude or an intellectual program. In contrast to the ephebic devotion of De Palma, this extraordinary responsiveness had nothing intentionally faithful about it, but neither by the same token could it embrace the pointed infidelity of, say, Antonioni's revisionism. It was ubiquitous but unsystematic; and if the first of these qualities prevented Chabrol from ever *not* being faithful to Hitchcock, the second—for what would Hitchcock be without system?—meant that he could never not be *un*faithful.

■ ■ ■

When I attempt to inventory the Hitchcock references in *La Femme infidèle*, I am staggered less by their quantity, though it is remarkably high, than by their disparateness. I find now an object, now a gesture, here a situation or mood, there a shot or framing; one minute I am watching *The Lodger* (1927), and the next minute *Suspicion* (1941). I am reminded of the game of Hidden Pictures in which we find the horseshoe, the comb, and the banana, but these never add up to a picture of their own and perhaps even spoil the picture in which they have been discovered. Except that Chabrol never makes a serious attempt to conceal Hitchcock's pictures in his own. His citations may be sometimes subtle, but they are more often indiscreet to the point of crudeness. When the lighter from *Strangers on a Train* (1951) turns up in *La Femme infidèle*, it has been ridiculously supersized, the better to be identified. Often even bragging about how much Hitchcock miscellanea he had packed into a film, Chabrol is remarkably free of any "anxiety of influence" in relation to his great precursor. He lets the Right One in without disguise or disavowal, an influence to flow whither it will. But it would be a mistake to regard such apparent defenselessness as the artistic suicide of a director so weak that he does nothing but the Master's bidding. Too unruly to be slavish imitation, Chabrol's Hitchcockianism involves something more like wild abandon. The overproduction of citations is, of course, one sign of this wildness; but another is their underutilization. Clamorous but inarticulate, obvious but obtuse, they forego that momentousness conveyed by directors who keep their Hitchcock allusions under firmer thematic discipline. Think of how consistently De Palma's *Obsession* (1976) sustains its parallel with *Vertigo* (1958), which it follows as obviously, and with as much fascination, as Scottie follows Madeleine; or how precisely Antonioni's *Blow-Up* (1966) targets a moment in *Rear Window* (1954)—when Jeff compares two photographs of the flower garden and sees what his eye did not—as its object of epistemological reflection. Chabrol's proliferent but less focused citations never stand out importantly as an index of the director's intertextual intelligence; they do little but perform his crazed suggestibility to Hitchcock's power of suggestion. No wonder *La Femme infidèle* is thrilling: there is perhaps no scarier dimension to intimacy than this excitable state of porousness.

■ ■ ■

Supersized.

A bourgeois wife (Hélène) has taken a lover (Victor); her husband (Charles) discovers this and kills him; though he tries to cover up the crime, he is caught by the police. Stripped to its bare bones, the plot of *La Femme infidèle* is almost the same as that of *Dial M for Murder* (1954)—and would be exactly the same had Tony attempted to kill Mark instead of Margot as he originally thought of doing. But one need hardly insist on this hazy point; the film exemplifies its fantastic intimacy with Hitchcock in other, indisputable, and more concrete ways.

Charles, posing as a man of the world who knows and accepts Hélène's affairs, has been paying Victor a visit; but his affable pose eventually breaks down. "You look terrible," Victor remarks; and we see Charles facing a mirror. He is not quite looking at himself—his head is bowed and his eyes are lowered—but a certain tenseness of the ocular muscles suggests that there is something he is determined not to look at but can't help seeing in his mind's eye. He answers Victor, "I know." And suddenly, as if maddened by what his downcast eyes have somehow absorbed, he seizes a statuette on a side table and clobbers Victor with it. We are given only a second to see Victor keeling over before we return to Charles, himself tottering, in front of the mirror again. But now he is facing the camera rather than the mirror, and we have a chance to observe something that the earlier framing had excluded: a matched pair of pictures flanking the mirror—little pictures, pictures of birds. The tininess of these images is no obstacle to those of us whose eyes the lighter has sensitized to Chabrolian rescaling; they are miniatures of the bird pictures hanging outside Marion's bathroom in the Bates Motel.

Miniaturized.

And lo! Charles begins to clean up the scene of his unplanned crime: he wipes the bloody floor tiles, wraps the corpse neatly in sheets, lugs it to his car. He drives to a swamp, where he watches as the body sinks in the slime; its descent is arrested for a nerve-wracking moment, but at last resumed to completion. Perhaps only initiates will notice that the shot of Charles washing his bloody hands in the sink exactly mirrors the shot of Norman doing the same thing. But everyone will see that, for over twelve minutes, *La Femme infidèle* has become *Psycho*.

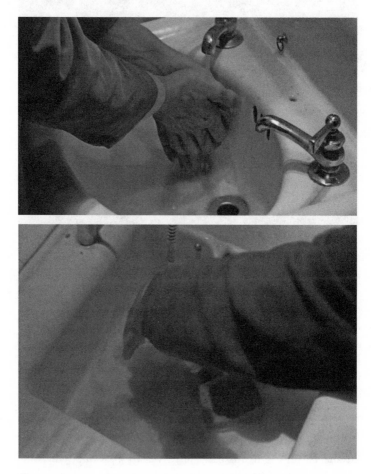

Crazy mirrors.

It is as if the bird pictures were a tiny leak that had burst into massive flooding.

For many critics in 1969, the reference seriously flawed a gem; too long, too literal, and too obvious, it seemed a kind of homage gone mad, and Chabrol, in paying it, a French Hitchcock

Crazy mirrors.

in the most epigonal sense. But the complaint ignores the genuine weirdness of the reference, mad to be sure, but also crucial to understanding Chabrol's process all through the film. For if everyone recognizes the extended *Psycho* moment, will anyone easily be able to state the point of it here? We know what Norman was doing in the scene from *Psycho*; it is much less clear what the scene from *Psycho* is doing in *La Femme infidèle*. The scene has become enigmatic in the transfer, where it plays out less as a glib reference to Hitchcock than as an unsettling Appearance by him, one of those weird cameos that always feel like otherworldly visitations. Even when this Appearance begins, it is too compelling in its qualities as cinema to be the inert plagiarism it was accused of being; if you could imagine someone who didn't recognize it, the sequence would not seem badly done in itself or stylistically out of place. As with Hitchcock's own cameos, it is only if you notice it that the Appearance seems not to belong.

And as the Appearance persists, it becomes still clearer that Hitchcock is not being faithfully copied so much as crazily mirrored. The drive to the swamp, only implied in *Psycho*, is now realized in a bravura sequence of beautifully fluent cuts and amplified by a traffic accident that befalls Charles en route. How much time will he lose in the formalities? Will the police open his damaged trunk? But for the fact it isn't in Hitchcock, all this would be classic Hitchcock suspense. Charles's digressive drive looks not so much like an original invention as a set of free variations on the source material. The drive itself obviously picks up Marion's from Phoenix, and the accident more finely extrapolates the swerving car whose headlights momentarily shine on Norman as he is leaving the motel room. Even the gratuitous cuts seem possibly left over from the shower scene, as though, not having been used during Victor's murder, they had to be used somewhere else. These variations are of necessity as tentative and tendril-like as the fantastic attachment I am trying to describe. It is in making itself so minutely pervious to *Psycho*'s influence that *La Femme infidèle* becomes its alternative reality, the Other *Psycho*.

This Other *Psycho* finds its most outrageous manifestation near the end of the Appearance. For Charles may not follow Norman to the point of throwing out the car with the corpse: the disappearance of the family Mercedes would be suspicious. Instead, he must remove the corpse and throw it into the swamp. But the bundle that he takes from the trunk is not quite the same one that he stowed there; it now appears chained to an enormous boulder that presumably will cause it to sink. But the corpse was put in an empty trunk that has never been opened until now. No narrative account can make sense of its mysterious boulder-and-chain. Yet far from being a continuity error—or even as one—this is the film's assertion of just how far its elaboration of Hitchcock can go. For in this air thick with transference, the bloodied boulder-and-chain is only there to cross-mirror the muddied car-and-pulley at the end of *Psycho*; as that pairing worked to exhume a body, this one will proceed to bury one. Chabrol seems unable to keep himself from laying on these "touched" touches, as though his susceptibility to Hitchcock accompanied him as constantly as—in the figure the film fantastically literalizes here—a ball-and-chain.

■ ■ ■

If only by accident of initials, Chabrol's porousness to Hitchcock conjures up Charles's porousness to Hélène. Though most readings maintain just the opposite, throughout the film this bon bourgeois has possessed an exorbitant receptivity to the vibrations of his unfaithful-faithful wife. On next to no evidence, he intuits her infidelity from the beginning; on none at all, he senses her complicity in his crime at the end. "I love you," he tells her in the garden when the police come to take him away; and her reply matches his in intentness: "I love you." No bullied "so do I" here! The couple share not just love but even the identical formula for declaring it; though consecutive and with a beat in between, their two "I love you"s have the effect of being spoken simultaneously. But then, wild as always, Charles's receptivity betrays him into adding: "I love you like crazy." To this Hélène has no response and drops his hand. He loves her more than she knows what to do with; at such a moment she, not he, seems conventional.

In the memorable final shot that follows, this scene of intimacy is replayed as sheer camera movement. Charles has joined the detectives who have been standing off at a distance, and we see Hélène from his point of view. Our remoteness from her slowly increases, suggesting that Charles is moving further away. (Unless he is walking backwards, though, Hélène is being seen by the Hitchcockian eyes in the back of his head.) Then, while the camera continues tracking back, it also begins to zoom in. As is well known, Chabrol set up this dolly zoom without determining which would end first, the dolly or the zoom: "if the zoom ended before the dolly, the despair of the separation would win out over the rapprochement; and if vice versa, he would remain close to her." As chance would have it, the tracking lasted a little bit longer than the zoom, and so, according to Chabrol, "the film ends badly." But in the light of his emphasis on being "close" to Hélène, which movement finishes first is perhaps less decisive than what the camera stops on: an image of Hélène through a grid of foliage, as if we were seeing her through pinholes. The image, far from signaling the annihilation of Charles's fantastic rapport, is the very emblem of its permeable condition. No amount of distance will disable his crazy responsiveness to Hélène; to the very end, she is seeping into him.

It is of course the famous "*Vertigo* shot" that has inspired this dolly zoom. How Chabrol must have loved that shot—how he must have loved it like crazy! For while Hitchcock's famous push-pull takes only a couple of seconds in *Vertigo* (and hardly longer in *Marnie* [1964]), this reiteration lasts a whole minute. Its length would dilate it beyond recognition if Chabrol ever played his Hitchcock game on only one board, but he never does: the dilation is another Hitchcock reference, this time to those long tracking shots that stretch out suspense until it breaks in discovery or revelation. Here, though, the suspense— like the love it depicts—is never broken or resolved. In thus expressing Charles's persistent intimacy with Hélène, the dolly zoom enacts *La Femme infidèle*'s other intimacy as well. The shot is a kind of paroxysm of that intimacy's combination of fidelity and free association, repetition and divagation. Small chance that chance alone produced the matching initials: a spectral Hitchcock hovers where the inscrutable Hélène stands and Chabrol's camera holds the place of Charles's steady but unhinged gaze.

Under the spell of this hypnotically long goodbye, wishing the film could continue beyond it, I find myself imagining a final reverse shot where Chabrol's camera returns to Charles. I can hardly say why, but suddenly I see Scottie standing at the edge of the bell tower looking down to Judy, who lies dead below. And I hear once again his wild outburst when he confuses her with her predecessor: "Oh Madeleine, I loved you so!"

10. *TOBY DAMMIT* (1969)

I FIRST WISHED for a DVD of Fellini's *Toby Dammit* in 1969, when I saw the film on its U.S. theatrical release and DVDs existed only as impracticable dreams. I wanted to detach the film from *Spirits of the Dead*, an anthology of European Poe adaptations where just to reach this version of "Never Bet the Devil Your Head" you had to trudge through the dreary wastes of Roger Vadim's *Metzergenstein* and Louis Malle's *William Wilson*. And then—more important—I wanted to watch the film over again, and in slow motion, and with the projection stopped at certain images and the reel rewound to particular scenes. For *Dammit* was a fugitive film: instead of unfolding before my eyes in the usual manner it seemed to be withdrawing—fleeing—racing from my vision. The images amazed me, but with the quick cuts, the careening pans, the ceaseless movement in the frame as well as by the camera, I got a distinct view of almost none. Now an excellent Arrow Blu-ray lets me correct for the film's infernal velocity, and I may scrutinize its images to my heart's old desire. Yet (no fault of Arrow's) the high definition proves not high enough; my made-in-house stills are all spoiled by some little blur or murky patch impossible to resolve. I must face the fact anew: *Dammit* is a film whose images, even with DVD technology, resist arrest. And for a second time I am driven to wonder why Fellini should have elaborated so extravagant a vision only to make it hard to see. What, after all, is his rush?

■ ■ ■

A quick first answer:

Toby Dammit, the eponymous actor who once performed Shakespeare but now only performs the bad-boy behaviors of an addict and boozer, has come to Rome to star in "the first Catholic Western," a parable of the Savior's return to earth as a lonesome cowboy. No wonder Toby has demanded a Ferrari for his participation! The already overblown conceit, described at length by the production associates as they drive him from the airport, will suck up the genre's other prerequisites too: "Our two outlaws represent irresponsibility and anarchy; the busty girl is the illusory escape into the irrational, the prairie is the region beyond history; and the buffalo are the means of subsistence for which man must struggle." To convey this relentless allegory (from which even the buffalo are forbidden to roam), the film will make use of images "eloquent in their poverty . . . a cross between Dreyer and Pasolini with a touch of John Ford." Poverty and eloquence are two sides of the same coin: by dint of their spareness, the images will have the enunciative clarity of pure signs. And as the reference to Dreyer and company implies, their march across the screen will be nothing if not measured.

While Toby is being told all this, the camera, aligned with his point of view, looks out the car window at the passing scene. In a few crowded seconds, the following images proceed and vanish before our eyes: a van with slabs of slaughtered beef inside; a lighting store full of illuminated fixtures; some construction work along the road; a fashion shoot; a religious procession; some Beatle lookalikes—to go no further. The dissonance between the film being described, with its minimalist images perfectly obedient to their function as signs, and the film we are seeing, with the opacity and clutter of its images overwhelming any possible semiotic obligation, could not be more striking. Against a film designed for exhaustive explanation, Fellini mounts the resistance of a visual practice that can only be encountered on the run. The breakneck pace forestalls interpretation by frustrating vision itself.

■ ■ ■

Dammit's commitment to speed follows from the swift dialectical vicissitudes of Fellini's style in the 1960s. In *8½* (1963), Fellini gave us a director hero who had "nothing to say" but wanted "to say it anyway." The film effected a shift from the art cinema's ethos of intellectual statements—the Something to Say—to the visual autism of a socially irrelevant but all the more bedazzling style—the Something to See. But even as Fellini was filming *8½*, the visuals of *La dolce vita* (1960) went Hollywood in Vincente Minnelli's *Two Weeks in Another Town* (1962), where the Via Veneto and the Excelsior already looked as clichéd as the Bois de Boulogne and Maxim's in the fin-de-siècle Paris of *Gigi* (1958). And after *8½*, the process of commodification only accelerated. Reduced to a name ("the Felliniesque") and a set of typical attributes (grotesque, dreamlike, virtuosic), the Something to See became little more than a way for spectators not to see it.

Under such conditions, Fellini's stylistic practice seemed condemned to either of two fates. One—represented by *Juliet of the Spirits* (1964), the film after *8½*—was a mannerism content to reproduce the reified Felliniesque in Fellini's own name. And the other—represented by "Il viaggio di G. Mastorna," the project after *Juliet*—was a failure to produce anything at all. What the fictional director did in *8½*, the real one did to "Mastorna": with sets built, parts cast, and a crew assembled, Fellini abandoned the film. On the originality of *8½*, he had found it impossible to build anything original.

Caught between reproduction and no production, Fellini appears to have thought of *Dammit*, his first project after "Mastorna," as an *exercise de style* that would mirror back to him his unmanageable quandary. In it, he says, "I was trying to mock myself—destroy myself—exacerbate 'Fellini style' to the point of parody and no return." *Dammit* would end repetition by repeating Fellini hallmarks ad nauseam. And since parody works best by abridgment—by leaving out the tissue connecting the tics—the form of this violent reprise would be a digest in overdrive.

The first three of *Dammit*'s four episodes reiterate—in perfect order, but exacerbatively—the well-known Silvia sequences from *La dolce vita*: her airport arrival and ride into Rome; her interview with the press; her appearance at a nightclub. Everything now has been cheerlessly routinized. On his arrival at Fiumicino, Toby descends no plane ladder, nor does a cavalcade of convertibles escort him into town; he is confined to interiors, behind glass. The interview, once live in a hotel room, occurs in a TV studio with the canned questions matched to canned applause by experts in white coats; and Toby's hostility to his interviewers, themselves antagonistic, replaces Silvia's happy flirtation with a titillated media. The nightclub, with a slight theme change from Baths of Caracalla to Hadrian's Villa, has become the venue for a thoroughly scripted awards ceremony—the Italian Oscars—abounding in phonies who are far beyond the reach of that ecstasy which once impelled all present to join in Silvia's primal dance. The "dolce vita" has surrendered its intoxicating sweetness to an irony as bitter as the whisky Toby half drinks, and half spits up, to go on living it.

As *Dammit*'s content repeats *La dolce vita*, its style is rehearsing the tricks and devices of *8½*, to whose virtuosity it adds a kind of coda. But in *Dammit* the virtuosity is squared, its execution quickened so as to outpace the speed of the co-optive culture in which it must move. For example, those disorienting pans that introduce us to the denizens of the airport lounge take the technique of *8½*'s spa sequence to a new level of *confusione*. This is not just owing to the pinwheeling miscellany of religions, ethnicities, and outfits. Unlike at the spa, it is no longer clear even what people are doing here. Though we might commonsensically suppose they are arriving or departing, the visual plan suggests they inhabit a more enigmatic condition in which no one is going anywhere. Sometimes, huddled in heaps, they seem simply abandoned; at other times, in urgent prayer, they appear to have taken refuge from the mysterious disaster (a storm? a war?) that the orange light suffusing the corridor, the strange wind rushing through it, and the brutal-looking mercenaries policing it all combine to connote. And though they're most often in motion, it is only to and fro, retracing their steps or even walking backward. The sped-up montage, as if similarly trying to avoid such a deadlock, only insinuates into the movement of images the same unbearable stasis.

■ ■ ■

The royal road for tracking this creeping stagnation is to follow the mutation suffered here by the Fellini object par excellence: the face. However eccentric, extravagant, or ruthlessly caricatured the face in Fellini had been before *Dammit*, it always stood in a classically expressive relation to character: its features amounted to so many traits of the person wearing it. In *La dolce vita* and *8½*, there were two kinds of faces: the generalized good looks reserved for the protagonist (Mastroianni), and the vividly exaggerated faces worn by the minor characters (everyone else). Both kinds were revealing. If the protagonist's face looked vague in its very beauty, that was because he was a "beautiful soul," detached from the determinations of a world that he preferred to sample (like Marcello) or soar over (like Guido). By contrast, the vivid "Fellini faces" went to show that the other characters *had* characters, at once richly specified and cruelly limited.

But look at the first face we see when Toby lands at the airport. It is the female face that appears as an image on a ceiling monitor. Its outsized, overcomposed features communicate nothing but the affable vacancy required to announce departing flights. The 1960s "flip," a barely softened helmet, echoes the bulbous shape of the head like a second skull. Along with the high Peter Pan collar, the tight round framings of both the image and monitor detach the head from the rest of the body. We notice, too, that these framings do not quite coincide. As if projected onto the screen rather than emanating from behind it, the image never stays put within the monitor, and (like the head on certain dolls) appears to bobble. Reduced to icon, function, "look," this face is anything but a window on the person, let alone the soul. And what seems most to disable its transparency is that the face is overwhelmed by the head.

In this way, the announcer announces the metamorphosis of the old Fellini face into what I will call the Facehead. Again and again, with inexhaustible invention, *Dammit* makes us witness the spectacle of the face—traditional sign of a person—being transformed into a head that seems only a thing. Instead of an old-fashioned expression, these Faceheads seem to be wearing masks that have nothing to disguise. The only mobile features among them belong to a TV interviewer doing facial exercises before her show and a performer whose rubberface is part of a novelty act. Some Faceheads wear actual masks, cardboard cutouts that render them two-dimensional in the strictest sense. Atop the Facehead, hair is lacquered like a shell or frizzy like a wig, inviting us antithetically to imagine what on many male examples has become all too salient: the bald or thinning pate,

Faceheads.

where balding marks the further advance of cranium over visage. And below, the neck has been lost to view through late-60s accessories (chokers, mufflers, Mao collars, fur pieces), oversized masks, or Fellini's literally cutthroat close-ups. Thus detached and unbelonging, seeming to float and turn in a void, the Faceheads offer so many iterations of the decapitation that will finally take narrative form in Toby's fatal accident.

Are the Faceheads human? Alive? At times, they are attached to so many prostheses (headphones, antennas, mikes, even heavy-framed or dark glasses) that they more closely resemble insects, aliens, or robots. And when the thick makeup does not make them look dead, the masks—like the Invisible Man's bandages—turn them into implicitly hideous survivors of perhaps the same unnamed catastrophe intimated at the airport. More object than subject, the Facehead finds its most evolved state in those wholly insentient globular lamps and monitors that decorate Dammit's world. The skull no longer lies discreetly "beneath" the skin; it has become the undisguised module for everyone's design for living.

Even Toby's own good looks—inherited from earlier Fellini protagonists—are spoiled by a truant eyebrow shooting up the forehead, as though he just might become a werewolf, a suggestion reinforced by his sudden howling in the car near the end. But he is more visibly in danger of becoming a Facehead like the others. His waxen, humid complexion already looks embalmed and becomes even more ghastly under the paparazzi's blanching flashes. Nonetheless, if his expression is sometimes artificially withdrawn or theatrically exaggerated, it still manages to convey a genuine struggle against the transformation that has

Becoming one of them?

claimed the others, including the usual female salvation figure who, though she never actually saves the protagonist, has always before (like Paola in *La dolce vita* or the water bearer in *8½*) radiated undeniable vitality.

Yet what point can Toby's struggle have? What authentic state would he be retaining or returning to? For the old expressivity now poses a problem, too. Toby's only emotion, after all, is disgust. He looks nauseous; and when he sticks his tongue out at people, it's both a reflex—they make him gag—and the expression of a project—to vomit right in their face (which is also ours) everything he's ingested from their noxious world. His quest would be not to recover full expressivity, but to enact a self-impoverishment that emptied him of everything including character-building disgust. It is essential to this ambition that, uniquely in the film, Toby has a personal demon: in the form of a sly little girl—a prenubile vamp very different from

Toby's girl-demon.

La dolce vita's "Umbrian angel"—this devil keeps tempting him to play with her ball. Toby's wild drive in the Ferrari will involve making a pact with her as the only proof of his having a soul at all. And though, inevitably, he must lose his soul, he gets to lose his head too.

■ ■ ■

In their satire of a late, "decadent" phase of cultural production, the first three episodes of *Dammit* make some claim to redemptive social value. Their rapidity in outracing a speed culture would be an attempt to get a critical distance on their subject matter as well as from it. But how secure, how stable could this distance be? Fellini's delirious tempo makes too good a fit with life in the fast lane; and the glibness of three cloned starlets making the identical thank-you speech is not so different from the facility of the perfectly matched jump cuts that bring them before us. Like Toby, Fellini is constantly signaling his own revulsion at what must be, sooner or later, his style's complicity with its revolting content. Recall the fashion shoot alongside the road construction: the auteurist brand ripped off to sell product. What can Fellini add, the first three episodes all seem to ask, to a world already nauseatingly replete with Felliniesque touches?

But the final sequence—Toby's reckless drive—puts all this in the shade. In a frenzy of acceleration, it takes the film's speed to the limit, surpassing anything yet seen in Fellini's oeuvre. This is the speed of nightmares, drugs, and car accidents spun into one. And Fellini seems to be looking not just for a faster form of virtuosity, but also for a purer one, one whose supreme velocity would transport the film from its sickening worldly content to nothing but motion, light, darkness: sheer cinema. Tellingly, the distinctive pans employed earlier for the passing parade of Faceheads are now used to negotiate depopulated corners when Toby makes a turn. And when the Ferrari is speeding ahead, Fellini gives us images of the road unfolding like a ribbon, so as to remind us that, like the car, the film is ripping up a strip. In the Ferrari's velocity, Fellini's virtuosity has found a new vehicle.

"Death to the Faceheads!" might be the drive's motto. They are sparsely visible here and only in their most drastically devitalized forms: as posters, mannequins, cutouts. The posters all depict heads being destroyed or effaced: one is coming open, another is all silhouette and a third has the lower half of its face missing under a mask. As for the mannequins, bizarre chef/waiter figures placed outside restaurants not even open for business, Toby smiles contemptuously at one, deliberately runs down another.

I misremembered Toby's joyride cum deathtrip as a single sustained race to decapitation; in fact, it repeatedly loses momentum and starts over. Toby winds up off the main road in a maze of little streets where he must stop, leave the car, ask for directions; and even back on the highway, he smashes through a roadblock, again halts and resumes. All these frustrations come literally to a head when he reaches a collapsed bridge. There, on the other side, stands the diabolical vampette who beckons him to come play and thus inspires his fateful wish: to drive the Ferrari fast enough to leap the gap between road and bridge.

By now we understand that far more tempting than the devil's putative pedophilic charms is the ball she holds. Smooth, without color or particularities, equally removed from the vitality of a person and the living death of a zombie, this ball is the utmost abstraction of the Facehead and—as such—its only possible alternative. When it rolls into the frame next to Toby's severed head, we too are weirdly compelled by the exchange of the Facehead's imitation of life for the sphere's realization of death.

Whether from malice or genuine inspiration, Fellini has lifted Toby's drive from *Two Weeks in Another Town*, but he alters his source almost beyond recognition. Unlike Fellini's Ferrari, Minnelli's Maserati is little more than the conveyance of catharsis: its roar is never permitted to drown out the more important monologue in which the protagonist (another alcoholic actor come to Rome for a film) talks himself free of his

Her ball: the Facehead abstracted.

obsession with his ex, conveniently along for the ride. Rather than killed, he gets cured; only his self-destructiveness is laid to rest as he resumes a successful acting career. It is not just that, by contrast, Fellini replaces cure with fatality; his emptied-out style abstracts this fatality from pathos and narrative rationale alike. Toby's is a sheer death drive.

Death, of course, is openly figured in the film's last image. One of Joseph Nathanson's great matte shots, it discloses the broody abyss that the Ferrari has flown over; on one edge lies the highway with its broken dividing line and on the other stands the bridge with its evenly spaced arc lamps. Not just the collapsed part, but every part of this road seems fissured, like the always-already segmented filmstrip that has effectively decapitated Toby by a jump cut between one frame and the next. In the obscene way that the thick reinforcing wires curl out from the break like shreds of torn nerve and sinew, the bridge seems less

Joseph Nathanson's broody abyss.

damaged than mortally injured, a metonym for Toby's headless carcass, which has presumably fallen down its cleft. This is an image of such radical stillness that, if the lighting didn't change from night to day, we could mistake it for a freeze frame. At last the film performs the pause function it has made us wish for and gives us time to look, contemplate, "remember we must die." Before the vision of what it would overrun, it stops dead in its tracks.

Yet *Dammit*'s identification with Toby's death drive binds the film not just to death, but also to the drive—not just to Toby, in other words, but to the Ferrari too. And, however memorable the matte shot, the drive receives an even more stunning figuration. Because of the placement of the decapitating wire over the far side of the bridge, we must assume that the Ferrari has succeeded in jumping the gap. Other circumstantial evidence confirms this. We observe tread marks beneath the wire,

Self-driving car.

and, though a mere falling barrel had made a dreadful racket only moments before, we hear no noise whatsoever, let alone any suggestion of a crash. Having made it across, however, the car seems to vanish. To those curious enough to ask where it has gone, the film supplies a mind-boggling answer. Earlier in the film, if we had eyes to see something besides Faceheads, we might have spotted a car with no driver moving slowly among the other vehicles in traffic. That buried image now comes into its own as the film asks us to imagine, as the very negation of image, a souped-up version of the driverless car liberated from gridlock and belting along an endlessly deviating road, truly death-proof. Unseen and unseeable, this image outraces all attempts to capture it.

11. CHABARTHES

CHABROL, *LE BEAU SERGE*;
BARTHES, "CINEMA RIGHT AND LEFT"

BY ACCIDENT

ROLAND BARTHES had a column too; it was called "Mythologies" and ran regularly in *Les Lettres nouvelles* during the mid-1950s. In 1957, the columns were collected into a still-famous book by the same name, but Barthes continued to write "Mythologies" for a few years after the book's publication. Recently, poking around in his *Oeuvres complètes*, I discovered that one of these late columns was on Claude Chabrol's first film, *Le Beau Serge*, which Barthes saw on its February 1959 Paris release and which I happened to be just rewatching in Criterion's crisp new digital restoration. I immediately "liked"—could not resist—the double accident whereby, having stumbled on an encounter between a favorite critic and a favorite auteur, I found myself viewing *Le Beau Serge* "at the same time" as Barthes. I might have learned of Barthes's column on *Le Beau Serge* almost thirty years ago when Jonathan Rosenbaum offered some brief extracts from it in *Sight and Sound* (winter 1982–83); but I did not, and having missed my first opportunity I was determined to seize my second with a vengeance. Since Barthes's essay was not available in English, I decided to turn over what might have been *my* column on *Le Beau Serge* to translating and annotating *his*.

"CINEMA RIGHT AND LEFT" BY ROLAND BARTHES

Thinking back on the first images of *Le Beau Serge*, I find myself again convinced that, in France, talent is on the right and truth on the left. The fatal disconnect between form and meaning is suffocating us; we can't get out of the aesthetic because our aesthetic remains an alibi for the preservation of the status quo. Our paradox: art in our society is at once the culmination of culture and the beginning of "nature"; the artist's freedom results only in a fixed image of humankind.

I would have given a lot to have amputated *Le Beau Serge* from its story. I'm not even sure that this story has a meaning for its author. It almost seems that the plot becomes melodramatic because at bottom it doesn't matter: truth lies in the style, the content being merely a concession. By a structural paradox, the essence of this narrative is nothing but an accident of its form; hence the total divorce between the truth of signs—the whole modern manner of looking precisely at the world's surface— and the sham of themes and roles that absentmindedly recycle the crudest bourgeois folklore from Paul Bourget to Graham Greene. Now, a nonchalant way of looking can give rise to sarcasm or tenderness, in short, to truth; but a nonchalant relation to the subject matter yields only a lie. No art but film could survive this contradiction for long. The ingenuousness of the theme would speedily ruin the modernity of the form; what's dreadful in cinema is that here the monstrous is viable. One might even say that at present our whole avant-garde thrives on this contradiction: true signs, false meaning.

All the surface detail of *Le Beau Serge* is dead-on (except when it sets out to render the story; the fake falling snow, for example): the fields, the village, the hotel, the square, the clothes, objects, faces, gestures, everything that subsists under the gaze, everything that is literal, everything that signifies an existence without signification, or whose signification is far removed from the consciousness of its participants. A fundamental elegance informs the film's whole beginning; miraculously, nothing is produced, except the subtle contradiction of rural existence, *pinched* (as it must be to allow spectacle) by the sudden arrival of a young bourgeois in duffel coat and flutter scarf, who reads *Cahiers du cinéma* over bad bistro coffee. So long as it doesn't give birth to the monster of the Anecdote, this delicate friction is exact, in other words, sensual. For my part, I would have gladly dispensed with the Sentiment; I would have been content to watch for hours the unfolding of this double existence sheltered in supremely intelligent signs; would have savored the minuteness of a description whose object was not the village itself (nothing more tiresome than rural realism involving a drunk), but rather this patient dialectic that unites the urbanity of the young dandy with the deformity of "Nature." In sum, what's good about this film is what one might

Soccer game.

call its microrealism, the subtlety of its choices; Chabrol has a power of *getting things right*. For example, in the soccer game that the children play in the street, he knows how to find the fundamental gestures, those that persuade us by what Claudel called the "explosion of the obvious." Formally—in its descriptive surface—*Le Beau Serge* partakes of the Flaubertian.

The difference—a substantial one—is that Flaubert never wrote a *story*. With a profound understanding of his purposes, he recognized that the value of his realism lay in its insignificance; the world's significance was that it signified nothing. The genius of Flaubert is the consciousness and the courage of this tragic deflation of signs and signifieds. By contrast, Chabrol, having put his own realism in place, proceeds to invest it with pathos and morality, in a word. whether he intends it or not, an ideology. But there is no innocent story; for over a hundred years, Literature has been wrestling with this fateful condition. With a touch both excessively ponderous and excessively casual, Chabrol refuses all restraint in storytelling; he narrates prodigiously, he produces a parable: *you can save someone if you love him*. But save him from what? What is wrong with Handsome Serge? Is it the fact that he has had a deformed first child? That he is a social failure? Or is his trouble more generally that of his village, which is dying from having, from being nothing? It is through the confusion of these questions, through the indifference to their answers, that art on the right defines itself, always invested in the separateness of human troubles, never in their connection. The peasant farmers drink. But why? Because they are poor, they have nothing to do. But why this poverty, this abandonment? Here, the investigation stops or evaporates; the peasants are no doubt essentially animals, that's their nature. Obviously, we are not asking for a course in political economy on the causes of rural poverty culture. But an artist should know that he is wholly responsible for the *finality* he assigns to his explanations. There always comes a moment when art immobilizes the world, preferably as late in the work as possible. I call "art of the right" this fascination with immobility that causes the artist to describe outcomes without ever asking himself—I don't say about their causes (art cannot be determinist), but about their functions.

The despair of Handsome Serge *derives*, in one way or another, from the overall social structure of France; that would be the foundation of an authentic art. And because a work of art is not a diagram, a balance sheet, or a political analysis, it is through the relations between characters that we grasp the totality of the world that has made them. In Visconti's *La terra trema*, the relation between the two brothers takes on Sicilian capitalism at close quarters; and it is the weight of an entire society that crushes the impossible love between their sister and the young mason. Since Chabrol has chosen to give his characters merely psychological relations, his village remains in the realm of folklore. It's a "human" drama, in a "particular" setting—a formula that expresses perfectly that inversion of the real which Marx described apropos of bourgeois ideology; in reality, it's the drama that is "particular" and the setting "human."

In sum, what the anecdote lets Chabrol evade is the real. Unwilling or unable to give his world a depth, a social geology on, say, the model of Balzac (the new cinema has only contempt for the "outmoded" ponderousness of *engagé* art), he nonetheless refuses Flaubertian askesis, the desert of a realism without signification. Too refined to accept "politics," he is too complacent to give an ethical sense to this refusal. The melodrama (the hackneyed episode of the snowstorm-cum-childbirth) is an enormous bellows into which he has puffed his irresponsibility. *To be good?* Does Chabrol believe that there is no more to be said if only one wants to be? It's when Chabrol's film ends that the real problem begins. The task of being good is not absolved of its modalities, which are universally interdependent: no one can be good *all alone*. A shame that these young talents don't read Brecht. They would find in him the image of an art that knows how to bring out a problem at the exact point that they believe they have done with it.

TRANSLATOR'S NOTES

1. Barthes's essay first appeared as "Cinéma droite et gauche" in *Les Lettres nouvelles* (March 11, 1959) and was subsequently collected in Roland Barthes, *Oeuvres complètes*, Vol. 1 (Paris: Éditions du Seuil, 1993), 787–89. Éditions du Seuil kindly granted me permission to translate it.

2. In 1959, this appraisal of a young director's first film by an intellectual who had just begun making his own name must have possessed only passing interest. Barthes's little-known essay was never collected during his lifetime, and Criterion is quite pardonably behindhand in getting around to Chabrol's uneven debut. But now that, over the course of time, Barthes's essay has come to register an early—and almost the only—encounter between two cultural monuments (the renowned critic, the legendary cineaste), what was merely unmomentous then must strike *us* as monumentally disappointing. The two brilliant figures, alas, met when neither was looking his best. If only Chabrol had been the Chabrol of *La Femme infidèle* or *La Cérémonie*; or if only Barthes had already written *A Lover's Discourse* or *Camera Lucida*; then perhaps the critic would have recognized in the director another supreme analyst–practitioner of the unbearable porousness of intimate relations (see my earlier column on Chabrol's *La Femme infidèle*).

3. Chabrol would have been the first to concur with Barthes's judgment on *Le Beau Serge*, harsh as it is; he quickly came to say the same things about the film himself: it was "stupid," and "its realist side" all that genuinely redeemed it. And as it happened, he *was* the first to concur, having rejected *Serge's*

redemptive theatrics before Barthes had written even a word against them. For on the very day that "Cinema Right and Left" appeared, Chabrol's second film, *Les Cousins*, premiered on the Champs Elysées a couple of blocks down from where *Le Beau Serge* had been playing for a month. In this second film, Chabrol abandoned the Catholic humanism that irritated Barthes in the first, while retaining the wildly transferential intimacy—here configured as cousinhood rather than friendship—between the two protagonists, who, to drive the revisionist point home, were played by the same actors (Gérard Blin and Jean-Claude Brialy) used for Handsome Serge and what British English allows us to call his "mate," the bourgeois intellectual François.

4.   Unlike Barthes's other mythologies, which either pitilessly lacerate their objects, or (more rarely) celebrate their charm, this one displays an ambivalence thanks to which its final dismissal of the film's rhetorical swelling cranks out some comparably willful oompah: Visconti as an example of Brechtian cinema? It is as if nothing less vehement could muffle Barthes's exceeding delight in the film's descriptive surface. "Personally, I could have watched it forever": is there a more unequivocal sign of fascination, of the essentially imaginary quality of what is somewhat disingenuously called "microrealism"? Speaking in a subjective voice, and moved by a desire to *remake* the film—dispensing with the Sentiment, amputating the Anecdote—Barthes is manifestly engaged in a *fantasmatic* activity, in protecting what is perhaps better named his own private Chabrol.

In doing so, he makes several striking mistakes, which only confirm the depth of his psychic investment. He collapses "what

Glasses = the intellectual.

Cahiers du cinéma = the cinephile.

Swiss tag = the tubercular.

is good" in the film into its "first images," its elegant pre-narra-
tive "beginning"; it is there, he insists, that the delicate friction
between bourgeois and rustic worlds is semiotically "sheltered"
before being spoiled by the story (*refugié*: an odd word to employ
for the function of signs, as though this function were to hide
meaning, to install it in a sort of Alpine hut that the French do
in fact call a *refuge*, where, in its gelid state, it would be safe from
melting into expressivity). But the children play soccer a full
forty minutes into the film, and the copy of *Cahiers du cinéma*
(on the cover: Juliette Greco in *The Sun Also Rises*) appears on
the café table almost twenty minutes after that. The film Barthes says he could have watched "for hours," he *did* watch for
one hour at least. And conversely, in his recollection, the film
he must have enjoyed during this hour lasted for no more than

a few minutes. It is as though there were something *punctual* about the pleasure he takes in the film: some single, half-traumatic, half-jouissant event that he is reluctant to see rise from the microrealist flatlands of insignificance to the embarrassingly explicit emotional peaks of melodrama. We cannot of course know what this event might be—being imaginary, it is perforce enigmatic—but some of the psychobiographical elements it picks up on are not, as Poe might say, "beyond *all* conjecture." Since those first images that Barthes begins by recalling contain no soccer game, no *Cahiers*, and not even a duffle coat, it is worthwhile to ask: what *do* they show? Nothing, it seems, but the passage of a bus along a country road and, projected over a single piece of luggage strapped to the roof rack, the credits. What has Barthes seen in them?

5. En route to an answer, let me note that Barthes turned to *Le Beau Serge* a second time in a 1960 essay entitled "The Problem of Signification in Cinema." Speaking there of how François's social position is signified in the film (glasses = the intellectual, *Cahiers* = the cinephile) he once again praises the elegant manner in which Chabrol's signifiers escape rhetorical emphasis. But in this "visual lexicon," as he calls it, Barthes lists one item that goes unmentioned in "Cinema Right and Left," though it belongs—and belongs only—to the film's first images. This is a Swiss tag on François's luggage. To see the tag at all requires sharp eyes, since it is hidden under the credits, but it owes to the same fact a certain semiotic privilege. For if we do notice it, it is together with the words of the title, *Le Beau Serge*; and this juxtaposition of Serge's literal epithet and François's not-just-literal baggage is our first instance of the delicate friction

between the "handsome" peasant farmer, with his intimidating but sexually thrilling brutality, and the frail bourgeois intellectual who has been recently residing in a sanatorium for tuberculars. For it is François' ill health that the Swiss tag (in this, very different from his Camille-like coughing in the snow) signifies with such admirable discretion.Barthes treats the sign to an even greater discretion as a reminder of the sanatoria (one in Leysin) to which another frail bourgeois intellectual—himself—lost a whole decade of *his* youth; in *Le Beau Serge*, François can at least compensate for former deprivation by adopting adolescent fashions (the flutter scarf), but in "Cinema Right and Left," Barthes cannot even utter the word "young" without edging it with a sour sarcasm ("young talents," "young bourgeois"). This is the *cousinage* that he might have recognized—and that his text, as if possessed of the psychic porosity of a Chabrolian character, or a Barthesian son, *is* expressing despite itself. In Barthes's later thought, the Flaubertian "desert of signification" will evolve into the precious muting of meaning that he calls the Neuter; likewise, the photographic particulars he singles out here (the Swiss tag, the flutter scarf, the soccer game) are destined to be refined into the cognitively futile, but emotionally piercing, details he will name punctums, those unpredictable prickings that stab at what, for lack of a better word, we call the heart.

6. Barthes was no doubt prompted to offer his glibly concluding Marxist dicta by the same motive that impelled Chabrol to end his film with a facile religious melodrama of suffering and redemption; flashing such union cards—*Les Lettres nouvelles* in one case, *Témoignage chrétien* in the other—is perhaps the *real* necessity imposed on young talents, who thus shelter

what might otherwise be spurned as an insufficiently socialized originality. To the early Barthes, taking positions on the left offered the security of being *in the right*; hence the compact, complacent, Voltaire-like tone of *Mythologies*; but hence, too, the militantly suppressed vulnerability whose release will be responsible for the anguished tonalities of his greatest work. That release is anticipated in "Cinema Right and Left." The essay disappoints only because it fails to be a mythology like the others, straining to the breaking point a form that Barthes had both originated and perfected. Here, despite the difference of uniform so stimulative to militancy, Barthes lets himself be seduced by Chabrol into a strange and unexpected intimacy with his Other, a secret, shameful sharing that he can only express in the rhetorical swings from rapture to rupture, love to murder. He might almost be a character in a Chabrol thriller.

In the 1960 essay, Barthes adds this reflection to the inventory of signs characterizing François: "their unity lets it be understood that this young bourgeois intellectual is playing at a 'role,' with that slight emphasis on its signs which Sartre has analyzed in a famous page of *Being and Nothingness*, apropos of the café waiter." Already, on second thought, Barthes begins to reassign to François the bad faith that, in his mythology, he blamed on Chabrol; it would be only the *protagonist's* wish—a wish to act out the part he has taken on—that the melodrama is fulfilling. Already, Barthes seems to recognize the Chabrolian irony that betrays François's grandstanding as just that. And a good thing, perhaps, for otherwise Chabrol must have had the last laugh. The film's final image is a close-up of, precisely, Serge laughing . . . and laughing and laughing. At first, we understand

Why is this man laughing?

his laughter simply, as an overflow of joy (the second son is born healthy), the laughter of one who has been "saved." But in its unusual prolongation, it becomes more akin to the hysterics of a madman; and as the image blurs and blanches, even the Handsome Serge (whose teeth are a bit too prominent for this treatment) morphs into a death's head, in anticipation of Hitchcock's radiographic rendering of Mother/Norman's grin at the end of *Psycho*. As Serge seems literally to have died from laughing, Barthes's biting question gets revealed as, also, Chabrol's: "save him from what?"

12. *MEDEA* (1972)

PASOLINI SEASON, Cambridge Arts Cinema, England, 1972. I first came to *Medea* ready to fleece the film of whatever gold I could get for my imminent Tripos exam on Tragedy. But the viewing was worse than a waste of time. Pasolini's film handled its narrative so strangely that, far from refreshing my memory as desired, it obliged me, back in my rooms, to clear my head by rereading Euripides and H. D. F. Kitto. And even this renewed concentration would be periodically interrupted by unbidden reverie on the very incidents and images I had resected, now scattered across my mind like limbs in a sparagmos, the still-bleeding evidence of what I had been compelled to sacrifice. Rewatching the film in two recent DVD editions, I see that, unwillingly, I had been a better spectator than I realized; Pasolini's *Medea* is essentially the story of all that gets sacrificed for the Story Everyone Knows to get told.

For there is no chance that so culturally central a story could not get told by any film that took it up; even in an art film hell-bent on muddling it, it could hardly fail to recompose itself as the cynosure of interest. Hence Pasolini makes no attempt to avoid the narrativity inherent in this archetypal myth; its key events—Medea's irresistible passion for Jason, his venal betrayal, her infanticidal revenge—are all present and sequentially accounted for. Yet, for long stretches, as every viewer recognizes, the film is bewildering, almost unfathomable, as if its director's cherished vision of a "cinema of poetry" depended on spoiling the cinema of narrative after all.

Why? Because Pasolini's decision to retell the Medea legend goes hand in hand with a refusal to tell it well. His style has no truck with established techniques of foreshadowing and suspense; and because it never bothers to differentiate essential plot functions from the inessential filler between them, every incident and image appear at once necessary, like the former, and arbitrary, like the latter. We follow Medea's twice-told tale through a constant game of catch-up: attempting to figure out in the light of later developments what we first saw without comprehension. "Seeing first, knowing later" is how John David Rhodes puts it in his essay for the BFI edition.

While Pasolini occasionally omits events (his Medea goes unrescued by the Sun God), or doubles them (Glauké, Jason's new love, dies twice, in two different ways), he typically adds new ones. Jason is given a prologue in which a tutelary centaur describes for him a sacred and mythical lost paradise; and Medea gets a backstory in her native Colchis to situate her in just such an archaic Eden. But it is not these major amplifications, however heavily intellectualized via Eliade and Fraser, that produce narrative confusion; if anything, they work to destine Jason and Medea for one another. More troubling—and interesting—are the minor inserts, the tiny incidents composed of only suggestively linked images or an enigmatic play of glances. These incidents seem so unimportant to the Story Everyone Knows that, far from being mined for meaning like the longer-sustained additions, virtually all of them get forgotten in the film's critical analysis. With the exiguous, irrelevant status of motes in a sunbeam, they nonetheless enjoy a similarly pesky visibility. It is precisely as peripheral not-quite stories sloughed off by the story at the core that they mount a protest against its diva-like centrality.

■ ■ ■

The poster boy for these not-quite stories is Absyrtus (Sergio Tramonti), son of Colchis's King Aeetes and younger brother of Medea (so much younger that he could be her son too). Amid the inscrutable Colchians assembling for solemn worship, his face stands out less for his beauty (though this is extraordinary) than for its unique inwardness. Moody as a modern adolescent, with downcast eyes and the trace of a smile—or is it a wince?—on his lips, he withdraws from the others to sit pensive under a tree. As he lowers his eyes, the camera cuts up to Colchis's troglodytic cave dwellings in which we see another, even more rivetingly beautiful young man. True, this one, instead of sulking handsomely beneath a tree, hangs insentient from a crossbeam; but his only garment, a low-worn loincloth, occupies the

Absyrtus's reverie.

center of the frame and the cave alike. We naturally surmise that this second man is the object of the first one's contemplation, as both men are of our own. But the reverse shot changes everything: we behold, not Absyrtus brooding still, but a woman, till now unseen, looking up at the hung and hanging youth. Recognizing her at once as Maria Callas, we are as shocked as the chorus in Cherubini's opera when the mystery woman in Act One takes off her veil: "Ah! Medea!"

Medea's gaze.

But not for the same reason: unlike Cherubini's Medea, who comes onstage as an obviously masked version of her own legend, Pasolini's Medea first appears as the replacement for another character, a too-beautiful, too-sensitive young man whose inchoate story she cuts short, as if pushing him off-screen. Her first action, purely cinematic, is to usurp her

brother's subjective focus, substituting her piercing gaze for his
dreamy look. And as if that gaze were as literally piercing as a
knife, its object, roused from torpor, twists and moans in agony.
With Medea on hand to preside, the ceremony that Absyrtus
had withdrawn from, and that the film too was putting on hold,
begins in earnest. We learn, almost redundantly, that the pen-
dent youth is Moriturus-elect in a ritual human sacrifice. As he
is brought into the blazing white sun of Colchis, we have an
even better opportunity to admire this model of Mediterranean
design, except that, regrettably, his loincloth is now covered over
with a sheaf of grain, an anticipatory symbolic transformation
of his load into good agricultural seed. Medea's gods apparently
deserve only the best, but being moviegoers and not Colchians,
we are more inclined to think what melancholy Prince Absyrtus
must be thinking as well: what a waste!

As the rite begins, Moriturus and Absyrtus exchange a series
of suggestive glances that revivify our conjectures of a certain
something between them. Moriturus smiles broadly; Absyrtus
half-smiles back; Moriturus turns perplexed; Absyrtus looks
concerned. But, in stark contrast, Medea's gaze, pinioning the
boy once more, puts a decisive end to this sideshow, a diversion
from her thus reaffirmed narrative entitlement. Having thrust
Moriturus into throes of agony before, her gaze is now as good
as a death blow; in lieu of the reverse shot denied him, we see
the tau cross that is the site of his death and dismemberment.

And Absyrtus's own narrative subjection to Medea is likewise taken to the limit when the two of them, having together
stolen the fleece, meet up with Jason's camp. First, the camera shows Jason (Giuseppe Gentile) looking at both siblings

The tau cross.

upright in their chariot. Next, it gives us a close-up of the sister looking at him, followed by a reverse shot of him looking back. And finally, it appears to begin a matching alternation involving the brother. But though Absyrtus gets his close-up, in which he smiles a tentative greeting, it receives no return; Jason's eyes, hands, are on the fleece. Absyrtus is thus cut out of the picture even before, with no other warning but a reverse shot that isn't there, Medea literally hacks him to pieces.

This is the trouble with Rhodes's elegant formula: what keeps "knowing later" from being satisfactory knowledge is that too often it aborts the nascent understandings that "seeing first" has engendered. No doubt, we later do come to know that Absyrtus's unexpected slaughter was simply a way for quick-thinking Medea to delay her father's army, which piously pauses in its pursuit to gather up disjecta membra; but such knowledge can never un-see the counternarrative it lops off. Could Medea's

axe-murdering of Absyrtus illustrate any of Wayne Koesten-
baum's twelve tickled-pink ways of understanding the gay Callas cult? Though a mother's son with the best of us, Pasolini has
hit on an unlucky thirteenth: his Medea-as-diva is the scourge
of all love that doesn't take her as its object. From our enchantment with the prima donna as our sympathetic proxy, he awak-
ens us to the violence against us by which she grabs hold of this
representational privilege.

While the not-quite stories of Moriturus, of Absyrtus, of
Moriturus and Absyrtus, get thrown under the bus, Medea's chariot rolls on, identical to the narrative's forward advance. Yet even
left *en l'air*, these not-quite stories take a certain obscure revenge;
it is largely thanks to their intrusion that the narrative becomes
both diffuse and clotted, "badly told." And by making a hash of
the Story Everyone Knows, they show it butchering them. But
"show" may not be the right word for so discreet a demonstration;
what is shown, at any rate, never gets said. Given how vociferous
Pasolini is in embracing the film's other polemic against the sec-
ular, patriarchal, capitalist First World that has claimed Medea
as its tragic victim, the prosecution of his queer quarrel with the
heroine manifests a strange reticence. Somehow, it is of peculiar
importance to the quarrel's unfolding that this Butcher of Boys
herself never be severed from their attachment to her.

■ ■ ■

Even less forthcoming than Pasolini's narrative practice of
linking images into a no-more-than-suggestive Incident is
his non-narrative practice of isolating the single image as a

Larva-men

no-less-than-impenetrable Still Life. This Still Life takes two
main forms, both of which have preponderantly male objects:
the frontal close-up and the clump-shot of inanimate or barely
moving groups. The frontal close-up is anything but the classic
window on a character's soul. We rarely know what its subjects
are looking at, since the reverse shot is ambiguous or missing

altogether; even when we do, we still don't know how they are looking at it. Built into the visual attention we are compelled to give Medea, Jason, and Glauké is a frustrated sense that it will never get us past their respective masks as sacred icon, celebrity pinup, and textbook catatonic. And these great stone faces are even more impressive when they belong to unimportant figures—a Colchian guard, an Argonaut, a daughter of Pelias—whose narrative expendability is at odds with their precisely detailed materiality. As for the clump-shots (as wonderfully mannered in their disposition of bodies as anything in Pontormo), they work to the same dead end. In most narrative cinema they would be the suspenseful prologue to violent action. Though once or twice Pasolini's silent assemblies do so explode—the Colchians in carnivalesque riot after the sacrifice, the Argonauts looting Colchis—these are rule-corroborating anomalies. Like the extras hired to play them, the men look awkward, barely competent at their appointed ceremonial or colonialist tasks. They seem most themselves on idle, letting Medea do her crazy thing while they hang out in an enduring—and often rather endearing—state of latency.

■ ■ ■

Latency: perhaps that is why the obvious "homo" coloration suffusing Still Life and Incident alike defies articulation in the obvious ways. In the case of the Incident, boosting this coloration into an aberrant sexuality feels as false as does, in the case of the Still Life, bleaching it into innocent male bonding. For whichever form it takes, the homo "thing" deters all sexual expression, gay or straight. On the one hand, the beauty of the attraction between Absyrtus and Moriturus is precisely that it remains within its own minor manifestations, that it *is* a waste. On the other, the ritual rioters are too concerned with spanking Absyrtus and spitting in the face of King Aeetes to bother fornicating with the women among them; and from the conquering Argonauts, these women seem infinitely safer than their jewelry.

There is something about *Medea*—something about Medea, too—that inhibits all sexual relations except hers with Jason. Even in liberal Greece, the sexes exhibit a remarkable reluctance to conjugate. Pelias's seven daughters are no more able to pull away from his magnetic presence than Glauké is to separate from her own beloved father, King Creon. As for Colchis, the kingdom may have devised a mythic way to ensure the regeneration of its crops, but it seems to have made no provisions, mythic or otherwise, for the reproduction of its citizenry. On the contrary, of the children sporting the same headdress as Moriturus, one readily suspects that they are bound for the same altar. Pasolini did film a ritual of "forced copulation," as if, even among savages, nothing less were required; but it only involves one man mounting one woman—everyone else, having thrown them naked at one another, merely looks on—and would hardly have removed the problem even if it hadn't itself been removed in Pasolini's cutting room.

The town's annual human sacrifice lays claim to immemorial standing, the practice of an archaic society that has no history but lives only in the mythic time of eternal return. Yet, as the centaur's inaugural lesson makes clear, the same King

Aeetes who sacrificed the divine *caprone* and hung its golden fleece from a sacred tree is also father to Medea, now priestess of the cult he founded. Thus, the would-be eternal order of the fleece is still in its first generation. And even before Jason's theft, this first generation looks like its final one. Old Aeetes and his queen comprise the only couple in Colchis. Representatives of an aboriginal humanity, the Colchians, without history or sex, also seem like the last people on earth.

■ ■ ■

Enviable Medea, then! She not only gets to have the film's only story; she also gets to have the film's only sex, the Sex Everybody Knows, while the hapless larva-men of Colchis and Greece are mortally sacrificed to the progress of her exciting drama, or else stand silent and shuffling in its penumbra, inhibited "extras" even within the narrative. But, of course, as we've been seeing all along, Pasolini's visual style is not interested in promoting the value of either the Story or the Sex that Everyone Knows; it is invested in dwelling on—or better, dwelling in—the impossibility of both. And, ultimately, it proves to cohabit there with, of all people, Medea herself.

The sex first. In Colchis, the only characters visually worthy of Medea (beauty being the basis for mate choice in Italian no less than in Hollywood cinema) are Absyrtus and Moriturus; her sexual outlets can only be incestuous or sacrilegious. All that makes the handsome-enough Jason a god in her eyes is the singular eligibility of his cock. "If you did anything for me," Jason later contends, "you did it for love of my body"; and Medea's first enchanted survey of that naked body—a head-to-toe pan interrupted at the interesting part by a smiling reverse shot and resumed below the knees—suggests he has a point: she has replaced the sacred tree with his adorable pole as the *axis mundi* of her new life. For us, of course, there is a further point to be made: once again, Medea puts a damper on homoerotic fantasy, not in the male characters this time, but in the male audience. She intrudes as the one who "naturally" gets to see what the pan promises and her interpolated image denies us.

Yet, for all Medea's invidious privilege, sex is a false lead here, and a failure everywhere else. Tellingly, when the pan shot is repeated after a later sexual encounter (with Medea now inspecting Jason in reverse order, from foot to face), there is neither interruption nor need for one: the man hasn't bothered to remove his clothes. For though Jason can hardly be thought of as fighting shy of sex like his farouche Argonauts, he accedes to it only having first rationalized it in the service of exclusively social ambitions. His wily self-presentation to Medea in the temple (from which, having caught her eye, he promptly withdraws, to let the poison work) has been pondered over in advance, like his later decision to take her in his tent; and he only cheats on her for a reason: to gain access to Corinth's throne. Shot after shot shows a long rope absurdly dangling between his legs like the downward-displaced necktie on a suit. If Medea sees what we can't, we know something she doesn't: his cock is a phallus, weighed down with all the deadly responsibilities of a pillar of society. Indeed, though a womanizer by reputation, Jason is never noticeably randy; if he winks, it is strategically, at princesses like Pelias's daughter or Medea herself. Despite

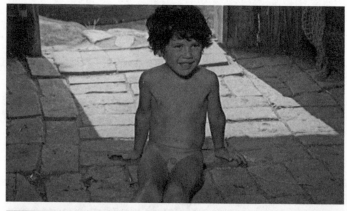

Latency, potency.

having two sons by Medea, his implied arousals appear to have been simply the outcome of a favorable cost-benefit calculation.

It is precisely because Medea enjoys sex—enjoys it ecstatically—that she is driven to such insane rage when its possibility is taken away from her by what is usually called Jason's "betrayal," but is better understood as the logical consequence of his Weberian rationalization of life. To add insult to injury, whereas Medea had been the only person in the film to "get" sex—to understand and respond to its ego-killing force—Jason will remain the only person to "have" sex, as another one of his prudently managed possessions. But Medea, too, knows how to calculate (an ability she appears to acquire at the moment she falls in love with Jason): if she can't deprive him of heterosexuality, then she can, by killing Glauké and Creon, deprive him of his reasons for heterosexuality, the use value that was, after all, its primary appeal for him. In this sense, the ending of *Medea* gives us the worst of both worlds: ecstatic sex and rationalized sex have become equally impossible, with Corinth now as post-apocalyptically bleak as Colchis.

On this annihilation of sex, the annihilation of story follows. Since the story has always been motored by Medea's drive to devastation, it is hardly surprising that the last manifestation of this drive should be the blighting of story itself. No wonder Pasolini had no interest in avoiding Medea's narrativity; he was counting on the fact it would ultimately void itself. The incidental waste that her narrative had produced all over its periphery, it now produces as its own peripety. For what does the classic tragic "reversal" amount to in this film except the heroine's undoing of her life's great adventure, her returning to the unstoried stasis in which she began? The undesirable, childless sorceress, having given up everything to become wife and mother, gives up everything to become the undesirable, childless sorceress once more. There is only this difference: the murderous rites of the primitive priestess had the advantage of numbing the anguish that now inspires the psycho-killings of an insufficiently modern woman.

Pasolini's Medea ends, quite explicitly, by going nowhere. At the close of Euripides's play, the Sun God's chariot—*deus ex machina* supreme—came to transport her to a new life in Athens. The elimination of the getaway vehicle here ensures the absence of any catharsis that would allow Medea, Jason, or any other survivor of the plot's cataclysmic events to "move on." They can only live on. Medea's last words, which end the film, curse her as much as Jason: "Niente è più possibile, ormai!" "Nothing is possible, now!" But English cannot render the force of that fierce final *ormai*, which, in manacling ora ("now") to mai ("never"), suggests that, for Medea, now is never. Now, her own narrativity occupies the sacrificial space hitherto reserved for Moriturus, Absyrtus, and her sons. Now, her story will be— and will be seen as always having been—like theirs, nothing but empty filler. Now, in her futureless fury, whatever larva-men are still standing may recognize their perpetual latency with a vengeance.

13. LAST TIME AROUND

THE BIRDS (1963)

WHEN I was fifteen, my luck at guessing Oscar winners won me a prize in a local newspaper contest, and I unexpectedly acquired a three-month pass to all the downtown movie theaters, of which San Francisco then had an abundance. At first, I wasn't sure what to do with my thousand-and-one matinées; my genie would grant my cinematic heart's longing—but only provided I knew what that was. Not until I launched into the *Film Quarterly* column decades later, with the whole raft of DVD reissues to choose from every few months, would I feel so flooded with possibility. I slunk from one ratty movie palace to another, sampling as many new films as I could—Hollywood, foreign, whatever—waiting for desire to strike. But on April 13, 1963, it became perfectly clear where I would find my gratis gratification. I would find it at the Golden Gate Theatre watching *The Birds*, which I had seen there on its opening the week before, *a second time*. "But you just saw it!": already I could hear my mother's reproach, but I'd take care she never knew enough to utter it. I was free now, free as you know what, to fly the family coop, with its restrictive viewing norms, and wing my way into the azure of Second Times!

That wasn't the end of the matter. *The Birds* was a movie that, as the saying goes, I couldn't get enough of. Already, in the first run, that meant repeated viewings and on-site research at Bodega Bay, where I saw birds nestle under the eaves of the schoolhouse, ate mussels at The Tides, and gazed at the "Brenner house" set, still standing across the water. And twenty years later, even the video revolution that let me watch the film as often as I liked did not satisfy me; my attachment demanded the security of a collection. I accumulated not only different formats of the film itself (including an iPhone download that put it permanently in my pocket) but also posters, lobby cards, scripts, publicity materials, and, along with numerous other artifacts and memorabilia, a *Birds*-themed Barbie, which remains in its box. At a certain point in stocking my *avarium*, I found myself acquiring duplicates, even multiples. It wasn't enough that my best friend gave me an autographed photo of Tippi Hedren; I was compelled to attend a meet-and-greet to obtain another from the actress's own hands; I no longer owned just one set of lobby cards, but two, then three; not only the original American poster, but the Polish, the French, the Japanese, the rereleases! And of videotapes alone, I had purchased a good half-dozen. As Cathy says in the film, about a man who shot his wife six times, "Even twice would be overdoing it." But what, exactly, was I overdoing?

It sometimes crossed my mind that, despite appearances, the possessive one in this relationship was not myself but Hitchcock's film. Or at least I detected a certain ambiguity lurking under the byword of my compulsion. "I can't stop watching it" did not just mean that I *wanted* to be always watching the film; it also meant that I *had* to be always watching it, whether I wanted to or not, that I couldn't stop if I tried. And perhaps, after all, I *was* trying. Had I been repeatedly purchasing the film in an effort to gain a purchase *on* the film, a literalized profusion of "*Birds* in the hand" that would counteract the hold *it* had over *me*? And was I replaying my other adventures in *The Birds* theme park, revisiting Bodega Bay like a poor man's Marcel returning to Balbec in the implicit hope that, after God knows how many iterations, they might take me, exhausted but assuaged, to an exit gate through which I could leave the film behind?

But though the old euphoria is gone, it is not boredom that has replaced it; it is distress. *The Birds* has become painful to watch; I now steel myself against images I once eagerly met head on. Perhaps this new anguish is simply the mature form of my original enthusiasm, which, like all love at first sight, prevented me from seeing not just the trouble to come but also the trouble that already lay, in germ, right before my love-blind eyes. What is certain is that, in a half-century, I became (as people do) a person who *has had troubles*, and now, when I watch *The Birds*, I can't keep these troubles out of the film, which seems to be not just recalling them (though they have nothing at all to do with birds) but presenting them a second time. And just as the film seems so precisely *reminiscent* of things that, in many cases, happened long after it was filmed, by the same token, it seems to *prophesy* worse realizations to follow in a future about which I am sure of nothing except that it will see the accumulation of ever more psychic "shit" on which, like a flock of indiscriminate scavengers, *The Birds* would come to feed. I foresee in short the day when my once-favorite film will have passed over into the domain of the unwatchable.

■ ■ ■

In *The Birds*, Hitchcock loads his cinematic images with one of the most insistent possible figurations of the state of cinema-as-flight: the birds themselves. These birds seem to be a very avatar of the unwatchable. For one thing, we rarely get a good look at them, as they rapidly flicker in individual or collective flight in and out of the frame; even "at rest," they quaver, fidget, and vibrate, unable to sit still. For another, they seem to prevent us from getting a good look at anything else when they are in the frame. They agitate the visual field, spoiling its clarity. The human actors in *The Birds*, their faces and bodies, have a composed, statuesque quality; Hedren as Melanie, Pleshette as Annie, and Tandy as Lydia are, for most of the film, pictures of poise, islands of stability in the cinematic flux. The landscape, too, is another such self-consistent icon: nothing is easier on the eyes than the shots of Melanie's convertible making its way along the eminently "scenic" California coast, under a sky in which even the moody clouds never drift. By contrast, from the credits forward, the birds enter an image only to destroy it. In their incursions into domestic space—Dan Fawcett's bedroom and the Brenner living room—the havoc they wreak on *framed pictures*, hanging uglily atop or athwart them, only reinforces their larger-scale attacks on Hitchcock's cinematic frame.

Avian anathema: framed pictures.

Destroying the classic clarity of that frame is the main achievement of the sparrows that fall—a paranoid would say dive—down the chimney into the Brenner living room. I notice in this scene how very much faster the birds fly than the humans run away from them, as if to signal the advent of a new sped-up cinematic pacing, one more aligned with the fleeting film strip than with the "natural" pace of human actors. And I notice, too, how hard it is to see anything amid these whirlwinds of small birds in flight. "Cover your eyes," Mitch tells the women, but the avian disturbance has already blurred everyone's vision. The women can barely see where to make their escape; Mitch flails helplessly with a cloth, unable to home in on a target; and we viewers, too, have a hard time making out objects and actions through the bird curtain interposed in front of us.

The clever ones in the audience, of course, see through, if not that curtain, the special effect that has produced it: you and I know that the bird flurry was printed over the human flight from it (Hedren: "All of us are reacting to birds that aren't there!"). And yet to be wise to Hitchcock's special effects only increases their great stylizing power.[1] His *Witz* here consists in coalescing two semantically distinct kinds of flight—flying and fleeing—into an almost Ovidian spectacle of mutation. We're not just seeing humans under a cover of birds; we're seeing birds *sub specie hominis*, in human guise. Waving their arms up and down in a scurry, the characters come to resemble big clumsy fledglings in their first effort to flutter. As the film goes on, this absurdist tendency to become bird-like—this "ornitho-morphotropism"—comes to mark, in little and in large, all human encounters with the avian kind. Visuals will encourage us to see claws in clutching hands and feathers in dislodged forelocks. To bring the lovebirds to Bodega Bay, Melanie has already color-matched her suit to their coat, and in this very scene, Lydia's coiffure, usually with every hair in place, puffs out into the wild form—irresistibly hospitable to the sparrows—of a nest. If this insane identification ultimately claims Melanie as its psychotic victim, that is because it is, at bottom, an identification *with* insanity. The avian essence in *The Birds*—hence the ultimate object of the tropism—is madness.

That is the gist of the swarming's incoherence. Though birds of a feather, the sparrows fly pell-mell across the room in suicidally uncoordinated directions. Elsewhere in the film, birds have an ostensible target, but the sparrows lack focus in this sense, too—prey to the panic and derangement that they inspire. Their confusion becomes almost poignant when the room is emptied of human presence, and they do not abate their agitation or take advantage of the open window to get back to their natural habitat. And at this moment when, in full delirium, they finally command every axis of the frame, something else happens: they turn into silhouettes, stark shadows that, depleted of earlier color and definition, portend a total blackout of the visual field.

But how this darkening frenzy does conclude is anyone's guess because Hitchcock elliptically fades to its aftermath: the sparrows' dead bodies, casualties of colliding with the furniture and one another, strewn over the trashed living room. Let Lydia alone grieve for her broken china. We spectators are nothing but relieved to see the debris; its immobility is a sign that we have returned to a normal, a sane cinematic viewing of persons and objects. And yet . . . that baleful fade! In a film in which fades

Ornithomorphotropism I: Mitch flails.

Ornithomorphotropism II: Melanie fledges.

The sparrows with no excuse.

Ornithomorphotropism III: Hitchcock fades.

are so frequent, so pronounced a transition, this one has the force of revelation, as it both cancels and preserves the monstrosity of all the flapping in the slow sweep of the camera's overlap. It is as if the film, bird-like, were flying over its own images.

■ ■ ■

But Hitchcock's birds not only make the image hard to grasp by flying across it; they are themselves disconcertingly hard to look at even when not moving. In this, they are poles apart from the dogs showcased at the film's outset, first in Hitchcock's Appearance with two terriers (his own) and then, as a kind of echo, in the sentimental painting of a pair of poodles hanging in the bird shop. One reason tradition considers the dog our most faithful animal friend is that its eyes so reliably mirror our own: its eagerly responsive gaze seems to confirm that it lives happily under our dominion as a lowly but adoring reflection of ourselves. And so with the dogs here. The poodles are painted so that their appealing eyes engage the viewer's with unabashed directness, and at the end of the Appearance, one of the terriers turns round to look, just like his master in other films, straight at the camera!

But no such mutuality of looking is imaginable with Hitchcock's birds. His aviary eliminates all birds with forward-looking—and thus humanizable—eyes; there are no eagle-eyed eagles, no wise or quizzical owls, not even batty bats. Instead, we have only birds with flat eyes on opposite sides of their heads; when seen head-on, they seem to be almost *without* eyes, and the cyclopean eye visible in profile shots is beady and soulless.

Hitchcock's dog looks at the camera.

The ocular creepiness spoils even the lovebirds. As birds who mate for life, "haven't done any harm," and are neither "too demonstrative" in their lovemaking nor "too aloof"—in short, as very different creatures from the *human* lovebirds we know— they conveniently idealize grown-up sex for the benefit of an eleven-year old girl. But with this notable exception: there is no eye contact between partners, much less any of that deep, tender gazing we associate with the *look* of love. Hitchcock's recurrent shot of the lovebirds in physical contact is anything but edifying: the tails touch—one is reminded of the vulgar fact that birds mate by rubbing together their all-purpose cloacas—but the heads face apart, and even if they did not, we could not envision them, or any other birds in this film, looking into one another's eyes. And since *we* can't look Hitchcock's birds in the eye either, we cannot imagine their eyes looking at *us* or understand how we (or our in-frame surrogates, their immediate victims) enter their

The look of lovebirds.

visual field. It may be overfanciful to imagine that these bilateral eyes must extend out and around their object like the jaws of a sideways beak—literally grabbing a look—but sometimes the birds actually *do* make a grab for our sight, as when they cause a schoolgirl's glasses to break or peck out Dan Fawcett's eyes.

All this is part of what makes the apocalyptic overhead shot of Bodega Bay in flames so abidingly eerie. As the birds gradually enter the shot, claiming the camera's vantage point as also their own, we grasp the obvious pun—this is "literally" a bird's-eye view—and we get the point (or a point, anyway), which is to identify Hitchcock's camera with the birds. Yet given how the film's imagery harps on the otherness of the avian eye, the apparent literalization of a "bird's-eye view" only makes us understand how thoroughly impossible the realization of this figurative expression must be. For what *we* are seeing from this aerial perspective cannot in fact be what these birds see, even if

"Bird's-eye view"?

we bracket their ocular peculiarities. *Our* eyes enjoy an exceptionally steady image of the town on fire. For over twenty-five seconds, Hitchcock's camera doesn't move, and, a bit surprisingly under the circumstances, neither does much in the spectacle below it. But the birds, diving up and down, right and left, all over the frame, can hardly share our static view. And their own viewpoint, if we tried to establish it, would be necessarily scrambled: some birds are moving away from the fire and would not be able to see it at all; some, gliding sideways across the screen, can be seeing it only with a single eye; and almost all of them are flying at an off angle to the camera's perspective.

If this shot wittily postulates a "real" bird's-eye perspective, then, it also makes it unimaginable—or imaginable only *as* an unvisualizable pressure that would subject our images to grotesque, unrecognizable distortion. Not by accident, the only painting to be spared the birds' mischief is the work of "modern art" that hangs conspicuously in the attic; its obvious abstraction, having already incorporated the birds' antirepresentational aggression, makes iconoclasm pointless.

■ ■ ■

So far I have been aligning *The Birds* with two very different versions of the unwatchable. The first version consists in the medium-specific fact—which the flying, fleeing bird-images never let us forget—that, in viewing any film, we necessarily fail to see a lot of it. But this is the weak, scholastic version of the unwatchable. When we call a film unwatchable, we mean something more visceral: not that the film images are too hard to make out but that they are too disturbing to look at. And we also mean something more intimate: not the forgettable normal condition of the general audience but the exceptional experience of that single, singular viewer who is one's own self. In this second usage, the unwatchable is always *my* unwatchable—as unique as my body and its psychosomatized history. Hitchcock's uncanny bird-images summon the unwatchable under this second aspect as well.

Logically, though, these two senses of the unwatchable, the visually inaccessible and the viscerally intolerable, ought to be opposites. If the visually unwatchable resides in what *eludes* our eyes, the viscerally unwatchable lies in what makes me want to *avert* mine; and if the former generates the shared exasperation of not being able to see everything, the latter turns on the private anguish it would cause, at a given hor-rific moment, to see anything. In one case, the film is in flight from the viewer; in the other, a viewer feels the need to take flight from it. *The Birds*' revelatory distinction is to remove the bar of this antithesis, to let its repellent terms leak into one another. Already the sparrow swarming has made us unusually anxious about visual blurring. And in a shot I now ask you to look at with me, the shot that most squarely enacts the film's ambition, it is precisely the frustrations of normal cinematic viewing that let Hitchcock elaborate his horror cinema into horror *as* cinema.

■ ■ ■

Now, of all the objects the birds break, the most favored by them is glass, their best window of opportunity being in fact the window itself. We see so many birds with their beaks, heads, bodies fatally entrapped in splintered glass that we might be forgiven for thinking that the bird war was being conducted against glazing. But, of course, the persistent assault on glass panes targets the human seeing that they facilitate and protect: the broken windows in Dan Fawcett's bedroom lead us straight to his gouged-out eyes.

The import of this nexus is the subject of two matched scenes in which Melanie watches the belligerent birds through glass. The first occurs when, during the attack on the schoolchildren, she escapes with Cathy and Michelle into a parked car. She immediately rolls up the window and, with us, looks out the windshield. Shots of crows flying against the glass alternate with shots of Melanie in frightened reaction. Yet strangely, if the birds *are* beginning an attack on the car, they don't follow through with it, diminishing in number and eventually all flying away. What deters them, we suppose, is the superior sturdiness of car glass, which is strengthened by lamination. Though Melanie has a horrifyingly close view of the rabid birds, this well-named safety glass literally shields her from being attacked.

The scene is essentially repeated when, amid another bird attack, Melanie finds herself trapped in a glass phone booth, which offers her, among other things, the benefit of a front row seat for watching a bird offensive that targets the entire town, and during her ordeal, Melanie sees some amazing, if appalling, sights *en vignette*, including a horse-drawn vegetable cart that tops off the sequence's overall surrealism. But nothing is more shocking than what *we* see once the birds' interest in the phone booth escalates into an all-out blitz.

The puncture.

In this doubly stunning shot, you'll have noticed that all trace of Melanie has disappeared; she is no longer on screen to mediate—to insulate—our vision as hers. Here, as the camera frames nothing but the glass pane, vision must be all our own, and with this spectacular bull's-eye, the gull seems to be attacking, along with the pane, the ever-sturdy camera lens that coincides with it. That no danger is felt to come *from the glass*, which does not scatter into pieces but splinters across its own frame, suggests that it, too, is safety glass.[2] (This is a leitmotif in *The Birds*, most explicit in the late shots of crows perching on broken, but not broken-out, panels of wire-mesh glass in the Brenner garage.)

Rather, the sense of danger arises *from the puncture*, the tiny hole at its center that threatens to let in what is on the other side. Melanie, when the camera returns to her, recoils as profoundly as if under a body blow; to *see* the bird strike the pane is

Safety glass.

already to *feel* it striking her. And then, completing the unwatchable's visual-to-visceral conversion, she turns away, stops looking. Hitchcock's birds, of course, often strafe without warning, and his staccato montage at these moments, matched to the abruptness of the attacks, virtually turns them into attacks on us. But if the shattered-lens shot strikes us, so to speak, as the culmination of such aggression, this is because, by figuring the cinematic lens as our not-safe-enough eyeglass, it threatens our most basic level of relation to a film: spectatorship itself. When that lens appears to fissure, the barrier that separates the spectator from the fiction and that ensures the self-containment of both is felt to split open with it. If we've been wondering how a bird looks at us, now we know.

Do we avert our eyes at such a moment? The shot, like many vividly memorable shots in Hitchcock, is brief in the extreme, and the function of its brevity is precisely to deprive us of time to react. Before we know what is hitting us, we are already looking at something else; the damage, of various kinds, has been done. If *we* can't avert our eyes, in other words, the reason is that *our eyes are being averted by the film itself* as it races on to the following shot. And the following shot here is exemplary in only seeming to offer relief from this condition; true, in it, Melanie turns away, as if for *us*, but only to face, as do we, more of the same: another bird smashing another glass pane. In this open assault on our point of view, we suffer the Hitchcock touch to the utmost: an overbearing, even unbearable, visual immediacy imposed and withdrawn again and again. Our eyes, forever being averted in cinema, can never be averted *for good*: such is the lesson taught—and the trauma inflicted—by the montage cinema to which Hitchcock has here maximized his allegiance. The visual unwatchable—the technical fact that our eyes are incessantly distracted in the cinematic flow—and the visceral unwatchable—the horrifying state of being unable to bear what we are seeing—have become impossible to tell apart.

■ ■ ■

As everyone knows, *The Birds'* outlandish fable has actually come true. Fond as Hitchcock was of insisting that his film was "based on a true story"—the invasion of Santa Cruz, California, by demented birds in 1962—even he could hardly have imagined that true stories would come to look as if they were "based on *The Birds*." But recent photos of a Syrian gas station under aerial fire seem only to have replaced birds with government warplanes and moved the site of human incineration from downtown Bodega Bay to the periphery of Damascus. In New Delhi, air pollution has produced gangs of sick, crazy gulls. And in Bodega Bay itself, the mussels I once ordered at The Tides now cook and die in their shells on the heat-blasted seashore. As current events—war, terror, pandemic, a burning planet, and the other end-of-the-world phenomena that are our daily bread—give its apocalyptic imagery a surreally documentary feel, *The Birds*, far from unwatchable, has become compulsory viewing everywhere we look.

But what I encounter in Hitchcock's unwatchable *Birds* is not primarily a set of publicly known events that the film might seem to anticipate. The first bird attack, resulting in a single small gash in Melanie's forehead, usefully isolates the essential

Syrian gas station, 2013.

Trump White House, 2019.

feature of all such attacks: *to prick the skin*. After the attic assault, Melanie's body, like Dan Fawcett's corpse and the Brenner house door earlier, is all over puckered with pecks. By literally getting under Melanie's skin, the birds succeed in attacking her experience of skin in the psychoanalytic sense too, as that organ of identity by which we hold the parts of ourselves together.[3] That is how the world goes mad on her and why, by the end, she can't distinguish man from bird, us from them, visual from visceral. Hitchcock has conceived the cracked lens shot—and the whole cinematic strategy condensed in it—to get under the spectator's skin to similar (if obviously less extreme) psychic effect. The shot does more than force an entry into our intimacy; it reenacts the primal gesture of intimacy itself. For every intimacy carries within it a whole defining history of such perpetrations—invasions of what we belatedly guard as our "privacy"—and our bodies house an archive of touches like this one in which, whether pleasurably or otherwise, we never had a say. It is to this helpless state of being handled that *The Birds* returns me.

Aggressively swooping through that hole in the screen, the film appropriates my every psychic tear, ancient or modern, as the "key" that makes its otherwise baffling allegory unbearably concrete. "Why are the birds doing this?" I don't know, but I do feel that they've always been doing this to me, or someone has, and I put my finger on certain sore spots where the birds, once again, come ripping into me. And the reverse is true too: through that same hole, my psychic life floods massively into the film-world, to get refigured in representations whose monstrosity, absurdly exaggerated, feels spot on. It is not quite that

Sister E, who slapped the glasses off my face, lives on as a crow, or that Father B, who obliged me to take long walks with him on lonely beaches not far from Bodega Bay, has grown a vicious beak, or even that I am the homicidal birds who take revenge on these psychic legends by way of Annie or Dan Fawcett. For when I watch *The Birds*, I can't take sides; I am too deeply identified with the interspecies strife itself, as a spectacle of all that is alien and feral in human intimacy.

There was, for example, a long period—coinciding with the years in which I wrote these columns—when my mother was losing her mind and when, in her presence, my mental confusion would match her own. If I found her pacing, I grew restive; if she was in despair over a calendar or a clock, which she no longer knew how to use, I lapsed into infantile helplessness at not being able to explain it to her, no longer quite understanding it myself; and when, inevitably, she began hitting me and I would restrain her arm, it felt like I was hitting back. It once looked like that to the well-intentioned passerby who immediately called the police. I never saw that ambiguous scene, but I catch a fleeting glimpse of it whenever I watch the attack on the Brenner house during *The Birds*. Lydia grabs Mitch's arm, tearing at his shirt; I can't tell whether she's clutching him for protection or assaulting him like the gulls who have just ripped that shirt; nor do I know whether, in removing her grip and returning to those persistent gulls, he is expressing the deepest tenderness or doing whatever he can to get away. No amount of viewing, however close, has been able to resolve these points. I can only assume that, as Lydia says, "this business with the birds has upset me."

Mitch and Lydia.

NOTES

1. To give another instance, the automated birds, such as the one that repeatedly pecks a child at Cathy's party, bring out the repulsively mechanoid aspects of *live* birds—and of human beings insofar as they are rendered bird-like in the film.

2. According to her recent memoir, Tippi Hedren did suffer a glass injury during the shooting of the phone booth scene. A mechanical bird, she says, "managed to shatter the 'shatterproof glass,' " and her makeup man spent several hours "picking tiny fragments of glass out of . . . [her] face." Tippi Hedren with Lindsay Harrison, *Tippi: A Memoir* (New York: William Morrow, 2016), 51. But lest there be any confusion, this injury cannot have been the result of the shot I am looking at. Here the glass, fractured by design instead of accident, does not fly apart, nor is Hedren (or even the inside of the phone booth) being filmed.

3. See Esther Bick, "The Experience of the Skin in Early Object-Relations," *International Journal of Psychoanalysis* 49 (1968): 484–86.

ACKNOWLEDGMENTS

THE "SECOND TIME AROUND" COLUMN was born from the invitation of Rob White, editor of *Film Quarterly*, and grew up under his inspiring discipline. Hardly less fortunate was the constant and unstinted support of Lee Edelman, Franco Moretti, and Garrett Stewart, cherished friends who time after time—after time—gave me the benefit of their resourceful minds. Joining this team later on, Ramsey McGlazer and Martin Zirulnik caused me to wonder how I had managed without their acuity. And at Columbia University Press, Philip Leventhal made this volume possible during an impossible time.

Many others helped and heartened along the way. I gratefully register herewith the Society of Friends of the Column: Jason Adams, Matt Bell, Fareed Ben-Youssef, Stephen Best, Tyler Blakeney, Angus Brown, Robert Buck, Frank Burke, Eric Burstyn, Frances Ferguson, Philip Fisher, Amanpal Garcha, Lalitha Golipan, Jonathan Mark Hall, Neil Hertz, Marianne

Kaletsky, Ben Kolstad, David Kurnick, Joseph Litvak, Heather Love, Laura Mullen, George Murdoch, Samuel Otter, Ben Parker, Kent Puckett, Hiroki Sato, Elaine Scarry, Anna Schectman, Joel Score, Elizabeth Simpson, Yoshiki Tajiri, Rebecca Walkowitz, Brandon White, Hiroki Yoshikuni, and Damon Young.

With twelve columns achieved, I'd planned to round them up to a baker's dozen with a concluding installment on *The Birds* called "Last Time Around." But I was unlucky. The Blu-ray release (my pretext) kept being delayed, and then, while I was tardily figuring out what to say about it, my editor-patron left the journal. For a long time, this unwritten thirteenth column nagged at me like a picture frame I had left empty. I seized a second chance to put something in it when Professor Motonori Sato—kindlier than he knew—invited me to lecture on *The Birds* at the Annual Japan Film Studies Conference in Kyoto. The final column, along with my introduction, appears here for the first time.

I dedicate this book to an enduring friend, Steven Ho; two such could never be granted.